FAR FROM PERFECT

FAR FROM PERFECT

A Short Memoir of Curtis Hicks

CURTIS HICKS

CHAPTER 1

Janice Marie Hicks

My name is Curtis Lee Hicks, and I was born October 12, 1973, in Portsmouth, Virginia. My mother's name was Janice Marie (Hart) Hicks, and I had a younger brother named Jason. We lived at 210 Project Drive in the Jeffrey Wilson public housing community, also known as JDUB. As a child, I enjoyed a fun-filled life. I wrestled with my brother and rode my bike with my friends. We often attached baseball cards to our spokes and rode around as if we were driving cars with loud tail pipes. Although, I was constantly falling on my back, I learned how to pop a wheelie while holding on to my handlebars with one hand. I was good; however, one day, I popped a wheelie and the bike fell on top of my head. I severely cut the back of my right ear. I cried, ran into the house, and my mother called the ambulance. The paramedics arrived and treated my injury.

My friends and I raced each other on our bikes quite often. We would line up on opposite ends of the park, and another friend would yell, "*Get on your mark, get set, go!*" Frantically taking off, we would race for about twenty-five yards. During the race, we would glance at each other to see who was winning all while paying attention to the finish line. The finish line was only inches away from the front door of a brick building. Often I applied my brakes too late and slammed my face into the wall. But I won! If I were not riding my bike, I would play basketball which would become my favorite sport. I also loved to play football, and my favorite position was quarterback. When we could not round up enough friends to play five on five tackle football, we played something we called "hot ball." Someone would throw the football in the air, and whomever caught or picked up the ball would try to score a touchdown by running to the closest endzone. After a tackle, sometimes we continued to pile on top of the ball carrier. One time my friends piled on top of me, and I could not breathe. From that point forward, I made sure that if I was tackled, I stood up quickly.

On Sundays, my mom, Jason, and I would walk to our local *A&P* grocery store. I bought a big bag of hot potato chips and a pack of Keebler E.L. Fudge cookies. Once we returned home, I walked straight to my mother's room, laid on her bed, and watched football and basketball. My favorite teams were the Washington Redskins and the Boston Celtics.

Another one of my favorite pastimes was to play five on five baseball. My favorite position was pitcher, and I threw a mean curve ball. My friends and I would draw the bases in the dirt using a stick or our finger. Because the area that my friends and I used to play baseball was surrounded by apartment buildings, we used the buildings as our measure for homeruns. If we hit the ball over a building, it was a homerun. When we played with baseballs, we would often shatter our neighbors' windows. This happened so often that our parents started buying us tennis balls to play with.

My mom spoiled Jason and me. If we wanted a certain toy, she would buy it. Even if it meant that she had to put it on layaway. My mother was a great cook. She would often cook meals that consisted of foods like ham, greens, and black-eyed peas. When we did not eat it, she cooked us something else. My favorite meal was hotdogs and French fries. She had a unique way of cooking us hotdogs in that she would place the hotdogs in a pot and cooked them on low. Right before they were done, she would place them in a hotdog bun, cut them open, placing cheese between them, and finished cooking them in the oven. I loved it.

My mother was born on February 27, 1944, in Murfreesboro, North Carolina. She grew up with her parents and siblings on a farm that was owned by White people. Her parents had agreed to help keep the farm running in exchange for a place to eat and live. Since supporting the farm was their priority, my mother stopped attending school in the eighth grade. This was what inspired her to ensure that my brother and I done well in school.

Janice Marie Hicks

CHAPTER 2

Churchland Elementary School / Fifth Grade 1984 - 1985

As a child, my mom woke us up every morning, and after we would ignore her first call to wake up, the next thing that she would say was, "Don't make me repeat myself." Walking with my eyes half open, I woke up Jason and stumbled into the bathroom. We would then walk downstairs and eat breakfast. Before I walked out the back door, my mom would zip my jacket up to the top, lick her finger to wipe the cold out of my eyes, and say, "Hurry up do not miss the bus."

I was in the fifth grade at Churchland Elementary School, and I really enjoyed school. I also enjoyed being with my friends, lunch, and field trips. After school, I completed my homework. One evening while doing my homework, my mom looked at me and said, "As long as you continue to do your homework, you're going to be somebody." This blew my mind because no one had ever said anything so empowering to me. It also made me care more about doing my absolute best at school. That year in math, we were learning our multiplication table, and as I sat in our front room studying, my mother noticed what I was doing. She told me to write down my entire multiplication chart. When it was time to go to bed, I folded the paper and placed it under my pillow. I then laid there and practiced until I fell asleep. I was not sure why, but I dreamt every night and I always remembered my dream. The next morning when I woke up, I tried to remember my dream. In my dream, I was studying my multiplication chart. I walked downstairs to eat breakfast and my mom quizzed me. I had significantly improved. In math, I began earning A(s) and B(s). But prior to this my grades had been average.

Spelling (learning *how* to spell words) was also a subject. Each Monday, I learned ten unfamiliar words. One evening at home, I was studying my words and their meanings. As I focused my eyes on the textbook, they became blurred. When I closed my eyes for a second or two, I could see each word and its correct spelling as if I had my eyes open. I thought that was cool and continued to practice that way. At home, I was spelling them all correctly. At school on test day, for the first time, I earned a perfect score. Afterwards, I began earning straight A's in spelling. Prior to that my grades had been average. I was happy and continued to listen to my mom's guidance.

Stock No. 03401800
PS-15-81R

PORTSMOUTH PUBLIC SCHOOLS
Portsmouth, Virginia

PUPIL PROGRESS REPORT

Intermediate

Year 19 84 19 85

Name of Pupil *Curtis Lee Hicks*

School CHURCHLAND ELEMENTARY SCHOOL

Date Entered *September 5 , 1984*

Signature of Teacher *Barbara Hamill* Grade *Five*

Assigned to Grade *Six* Next Year

Signature of Principal *Cecelia C. Curcis*

TO THE PARENT OR GUARDIAN:

This report is sent to you in order that you may know what your child is accomplishing in school.

You are requested to examine this report, sign and return it promptly. Your signature does not mean that you are satisfied with the progress of your child; it indicates that you have seen this report. If your child's marks show that help is needed, please contact the school and discuss the problem with the principal and teacher.

We need your interest, cooperation, and understanding in what the school is attempting to do for your child.

Rondle E. Edwards
Superintendent of Schools

MARKING KEY FOR ACHIEVEMENT IN THE ACADEMIC SKILLS:

A – Outstanding C – Satisfactory
B – Above Average D – Needs Improvement
F – Unsatisfactory

Front Cover of Report Card

5th Grade Report Card

That year, my mom started a business out of our kitchen. She began to sell small bags of popcorn, potato chips, all kinds of candy, sodas, sour and dill pickles, ice bergs and frozen cups, penny cookies and all kinds of cigarettes.

She purchased her candy from a large candy store in Portsmouth. At home, she had covered a small table with a tablecloth and placed her items for sale on top of the table. When it came to cigarettes, Newport shorts were our biggest seller. To store the cigarettes, she used a cardboard box and assembled shelves within the box. There were nine or more shelves, and her presentation was done very nicely.

My mother purchased her cartons of cigarettes from a *lady* off the streets. At night, the lady would knock on our back door and my mom would let her in. She would have black trash bags full of cigarettes. I would help them sort everything out. Afterwards, my mom would pay her, and the lady would leave. Daily my mom began to teach me how to serve customers and count money. Everything was going well until one night when someone tried to break into our apartment through our kitchen window. My mom had to call the police. Later that week, we found out it was a guy that lived in the neighborhood.

My mother was highly creative and produced different ideas to entertain her customers. I can remember her emptying a pickle jar, affixing a small cup to the bottom of the jar, filling it with water, and cutting a quarter sized hole into the top of the lid. The objective was for the customer to try to drop the coin into the cup. If that happened, the customer won something. Although I cannot remember all the details, I do remember customers loving to try it.

By the middle of my fifth-grade year, my friends at school learned I was the candy connect and I began selling candy at school. My mother's business had become very profitable. She was able to buy us new clothes, a boom box radio, action figures, an Atari game system, Playboy bunny dress shoes, Michael Jackson jacket and gloves, ten speed bikes, a large fish tank with fish so large, they often jumped out of the tank and onto our floor, and a bird cage.

My mother was also able to buy a life insurance policy and a small four door car. Life was good. We were now able to visit our grandmother and other family members that lived out of state. My grandmother's name was Vanessa Hart. She lived in a nursing home that was down the street from another public housing community called *Swanson Homes* in Portsmouth. She was a very loving person. During this time, she was eighty-five years old. It was always great to see my grandmother and I felt sad when it was time for us to leave. I never met my grandfather; because he had passed away before I was born.

CHAPTER 3

Murfreesboro & Conway, NC / Franklin & Boykins, VA

Every month, my mother began to drive us an hour one way to North Carolina to visit our family. Our first stop was in Murfreesboro, which was quite different from Portsmouth in that it was much more rural than what we were used to. About a mile from our destination, the paved road turned into gravel and rocks. We rolled our windows up as dust entered the car. When mom tried to park in our family's driveway, the uneven pavement scrapped the bottom of our car. Shortly after, a large dog ran to our car and began to bark. I did not like dogs and feared most of them. When my mother stepped out of the car, Jason and I stayed in. Eventually, my mother's sister Aunt Lauren and her husband Mr. Matthews walked outside and grabbed the dog. They were both older than my mother and lived in an older model double wide trailer. I remember Aunt Lauren being soft spoken and pleasant to us. Mr. Matthews also treated us nicely. They had a son named Lemon. We were close in age and played well together. Outside was a bent basketball rim without netting. We dribbled the half-inflated basketball on dirt and gravel before taking a shot. I had fun.

Afterwards, my mom drove twenty minutes to Conway where we visited her other sister Aunt Mary and her husband Mr. Gordon Cumbo. They also lived in a double wide trailer. Aunt Mary did not have any dogs which was a relief. At that time, they were both over sixty years old, and they never had children. In their yard was a shed with a metal horseshoe at the top of the front door. It resembled the one my mother hung at home. My family believed that horseshoes brought you good luck, so it was common to see one hanging around. Aunt Mary would let us in, and we all hugged, sat down, and talked. She was an easy-going religious lady, and I never heard her curse or raise her voice. She was always calm and often referenced the *Lord*. Aunt Mary also enjoyed cooking. My favorites were her chicken and dumplings, fried sweet potatoes, and homemade biscuits.

Mr. Cumbo was nice and joked with Jason and I. I was not sure why, but his feet pointed inward. He walked with a limp and used a cane for support. On this trip, he called me outside. I noticed him working in the hog pen. As I watched the chickens roam in the grass filled yard, I heard a pig squeal. When I looked over, Mr. Cumbo had killed it using a mallet. I felt sorry for the pig. Later that day, we all sat outside by the shed, talked, and waved at every passing car.

Mom talked about moving back to Conway and living next to Aunt Mary. I did not want to because it was a little too country for me. Plus, I did not want to leave my friends or the school I attended. My mom then began to talk about my dad named Malik Jordan. She said that he grew up somewhere nearby. I had never seen him before. She also talked about visiting a root doctor. I did not understand what she was talking about. So, my mother asked me, "If I remembered when Jason had bad dreams?" I said, "Yes." She asked, "If his bad dreams had stopped?" and again I said, "Yes." She responded with, "She used roots to help him." In addition, she explained how she used it to help me learn my math. Even though I nodded as if I agreed, I still did not understand. The conversation would change and shortly after we would leave.

We were off to visit another family member. As mom drove, she forewarned us about a bridge we had to cross. As we approached it, I noticed it was a small makeshift wooden bridge. My mom stopped at the base of the bridge. It was wide enough for only one car to cross at a time. Once our car tires rolled onto the bridge, we elevated straight into the air. Since we could not see whether a vehicle was crossing from the other side, she had to blow her horn as she drove over. If there was a car on the other side, they would hear our horn. It was scary but we crossed over and drove to Ms. Felicia Jean's house. She had a daughter, and they were both nice.

On other occasions, we would visit Aunt Blair and Aunt Patty Hicks. Aunt Blair lived in a town called Boykins. She had children and they were all nice. Aunt Patty lived in a town called Franklin. She lived in a big house surrounded by cornfields. When my mom drove to the back of Aunt Patty's house, two big German shepherds ran towards our car. A minute later, Aunt Patty and her daughters would walk outside. Once they locked the dogs up, we all sat outside and talked. I can remember one time I had to use the bathroom, so I went inside the house. When I walked out of the bathroom, there was a dog walking into the house. Scared and not knowing what to do, I sprinted upstairs, ran into a bedroom, and closed the door. Because I had feared that the dog was standing by the door, I did not open it. Instead, I opened the bedroom window, and jumped out. I landed awkwardly on my feet and fell on the ground in pain. I stood up, brushed off the dirt and walked back to our car. When I told my mom what I had done, she fussed and made sure I was OKAY. Right before the sun would set, we would leave and drive back to Portsmouth.

Weeks later, my mother again talked about moving to Conway. Since she had never acted on her thoughts, I ignored it. However, one weekend, my mother showed me that she was serious. We drove from Portsmouth to Suffolk, Virginia, and she bought a brand new double wide trailer. It was nice. Since Aunt Mary had an acre of land, my mother had it delivered and placed directly behind Aunt Mary's trailer. My mother planned to use the shed as her candy store. Over the summer, she drove from Portsmouth to Conway dropping off new appliances and beautiful pieces of home interior.

CHAPTER 4

Churchland Junior High School / Seventh & Eight Grade Years 1986 – 1988

I do not remember much about my sixth grade year at Churchland Elementary School. In 1986, I attended a new school called Churchland Junior High School. While my memory of seventh grade again is foggy, I do remember my friends and I watched and imitated a lot of professional wrestling. We began to wrestle against each other at home and at school. But after my friends and I grew tired of being jumped on individually, we decided to join forces and called ourselves "The Four Horsemen." We made our own wrestling belts using cardboard, glue, and glitter. They were nice.

I was not sure why, but the kids divided JDUB into two halves. It was always our end against their end. If guys walked down to our end, we jumped them and vice versa. There was not a wrestling move that we did not use on each other. My favorite wrestling move was the figure four. My homeboy, Terrel was the best wrestler out of all of us. He lived down my end. When we wanted to imitate cage match wrestling, we walked to his building. Since he lived near a baseball field, we could throw each other up against the metal fences and do wrestling moves. This was a lot of fun.

It was June of 1988 and *the end of my eighth-grade year.* I was enrolled in all honors classes and was doing exceptionally well in school. The district examinations I completed had ranked me amongst the brightest students. That year, I earned the Excellence in Science award. I also done well in math. On the day of our math award's ceremony, I was nervous as I sat quietly waiting for class to begin. My math teacher's name was Ms. Delana. She was Black and my favorite teacher. She began by congratulating us on completing eighth grade and explained that she usually only presented this award to one student; however, this year she felt that there were two deserving students. When she called my name, I stood up and smiled. I had earned the Superior Achievement and Excellence of Performance in Math Award. This was my proudest moment in junior high school.

SCA Treasurer 1986

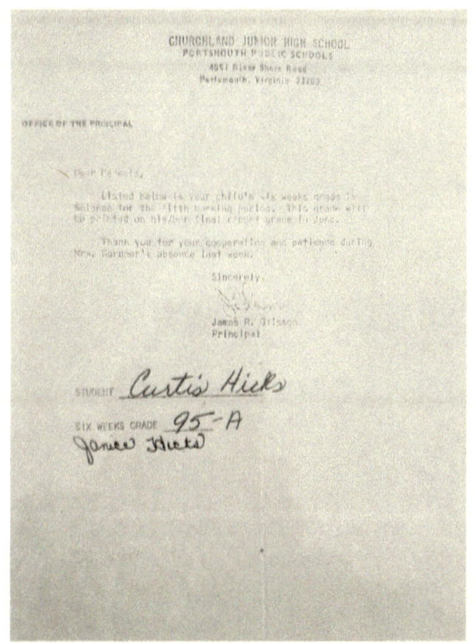

CHURCHLAND JUNIOR HIGH SCHOOL
PORTSMOUTH PUBLIC SCHOOLS
4051 River Shore Road
Portsmouth, Virginia 23703

OFFICE OF THE PRINCIPAL

Dear Parents:

Listed below is your child's six weeks grade in Science for the fifth marking period. This grade will be printed on his/her final report grade in June.

Thank you for your cooperation and patience during Mrs. Gardner's absence last week.

Sincerely,

James R. Grisson
Principal

STUDENT *Curtis Hicks*

SIX WEEKS GRADE *95 – A*

Janice Hicks

Portsmouth Public Schools
Portsmouth, Virginia

Churchland Junior High School

This certificate is awarded to

Curtis Hicks
for

Academic Excellence in Science
4th 6 weeks A

Principal *Robert E. Little*
Teacher

date *March 16, 1987*

8th Grade Academic Excellence in Science

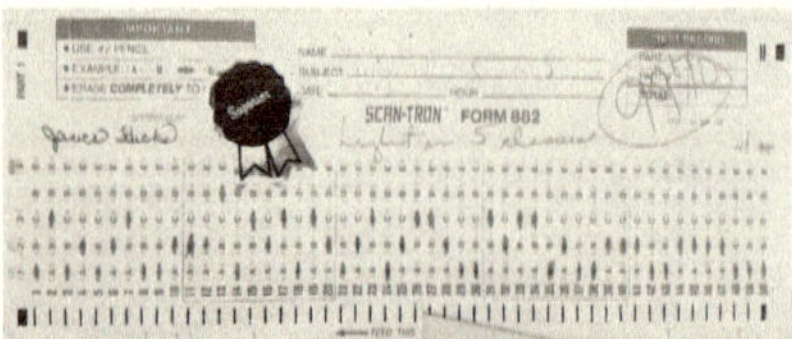

8th Grade Science

8th Grade Superior Achievement in Math

That summer was great. I spent time playing with my friends which was fun. In addition, my cousin Theo would often ride his bike over to visit us. He lived with his mother and siblings in the Ida Barbour public housing community. When he visited our apartment, we would all talk for hours, and when it was time for him to leave, my mom always told him to be careful while riding his bicycle in the dark. He was never concerned, but always replied with, "OKAY, and that his brother was looking out for him." At first, I did not understand what he meant until I learned that he had lost a brother.

Also, during that summer my mom drove us to Washington D.C. to visit more family members. One of our cousins drove us to The White House and to one of the national monuments where we were able to take a tour of both sites. It was a wonderful experience, and we were very appreciative. One weekend, I was outside playing, and my mom called me into the house. This was when I met Jason's dad Julius Hicks. Our mom had driven from Portsmouth to Boykins to pick him up and although I did not know him, I was happy for Jason. But unfortunately, for two days I watched Julius drink beer and pay little attention to Jason. I was glad when my mother drove him back, because Julius was not on our lease, and if one of our neighbors would have reported us to our housing authority, we could have been evicted.

CHAPTER 5

Ninth Grade Year

It was September of 1988, and I began my freshman year at Churchland High School. For the first month, school was going well. One Friday evening, my mother drove back to Boykins to pick up Julius. When they returned, again Julius spent his time drinking beer, and sleeping. It was Sunday night and my mom made us go to bed. As Jason and I slept, I heard my mom and Julius arguing downstairs. A few moments later, she walked upstairs, woke us up, and told us to put on our clothes. Afterwards, she walked Jason and I out the front door and told us that "Julius had pointed a gun at her and threatened to kill her." She said that "We had to spend the night with a neighbor." As we walked down the narrow sidewalk, my mother told us not to worry. She knocked on a lady's back door and she let us in. I do not remember the name of the lady we stayed with that night, but I do remember her also being a candy lady. My mother hugged us and said, "To go to sleep," but I could not. I laid there crying and worrying about her safety. The next morning, my mother walked us back to our apartment and we prepared for school. As I watched her, I noticed she looked sad and was not acting like herself. She also looked tired and confused. She told me that "She was driving Julius back to Boykins and was leaving before we caught the school bus." I said, "OKAY." I remembered looking into my mother's eyes before she walked out the back door. I felt as if that would be the last time I saw her alive. I caught the bus to school and tried to treat it like a normal day, but I could not.

As I sat in my first period class, there was an announcement for me to report to the office. My heart pounded, and I wondered why they were calling me. I thought only bad students were called to the office. When I walked into the office, I noticed the sad look on the administrator's faces. There were other people in the room that were crying and could not look at me. I was informed that my mother had died in a car accident (October 6, 1988). I remember crying and feeling sick. Jason just celebrated his twelfth birthday. I was thirteen years old, and my birthday was a week away.

Our next-door neighbor Ms. Sara Thompson picked us up from school. Once we arrived home, I found it difficult to exit the car and walk to our apartment. As Jason and I sat in our front room with Ms. Thompson, locals began to come to our apartment to express their condolences. While some of the women cried, others walked throughout the apartment and stole my mother's belongings. That night, Jason and I stayed with our good friend and neighbor

Cameron and his mother, Ms. Amber Mitchell. We were grateful. The following day, we did not attend school. That night Jason and I spent the night with another neighbor named Ms. Arlissa Blair. She had three sons. Although we missed a day or two of school, Jason and I continued attending school. Days after we moved in, Ms. Blair asked me "Who I wanted to live with?" I said that I did not want to live with my family in North Carolina, nor did I want to change school. I knew that we had other family members that lived in Portsmouth, but they all had children of their own. Then I thought about our cousin Theo. Theo was cool and we were related because his mother, Augustine, had married my mother's brother, William Hart. I said I wanted to live with Theo's family. With Ms. Blair's assistance, someone contacted Theo's mother Augustine and she agreed.

A few days later, my mother's funeral was held in her hometown. I really do not remember much, because it was a difficult day to say the least. I felt bad for my brother and my grandmother because I knew that they were both filled with grief. After the funeral someone drove my grandmother back to the nursing home. In a packed car, Jason and I rode back to Portsmouth. When we arrived at Augustine's house, I sat down and began to think more about my decision to live with her. This meant we had to change schools. Jason would have to attend Harry Hunt Junior High School, and my new school would be Woodrow Wilson High School. While Woodrow Wilson was a great school, I did not want to change schools. So, I walked downstairs and told Augustine that I did not want to change schools. She was fine with it; however, this meant that I would have to walk to the nearest bus stop zoned for Churchland High.

On Monday morning, I woke up early, washed up, put on my clothes, and walked downstairs. After breakfast, I sat in the chair trying to prepare myself for something I had never done before. I had no clue how long it would take me to get to the closest bus stop. However, at 6:25 a.m., I walked out the front door with my bookbag. Since I could see dope dealers and drug addicts, I knew I should exit the park as quickly as possible. As I walked fast and jogged, my closest school zone was in another public housing community called London Oaks. It was two miles away. Once I arrived, I was exhausted. I remember standing there and not uttering a word. During those days, it was not wise to walk through communities that we did not live in. Often guys were beaten up for doing so. Ten minutes later, the bus would arrive, and I boarded and kept to myself. I did not want any trouble. I needed to sit down and rest my mind and body.

When I walked into the school, countless faculty members and friends greeted me. It was good to see them. As the day went on, even though I appreciated the love showered upon me, mentally I was not there. When the school day ended, I waved at my friends on the Jeffrey Wilson school bus before getting on my new bus and riding back to London Oaks where I walked another two miles back home.

Augustine was forty-eight years old and lived in a two-bedroom one bathroom apartment with her five adult children. My uncle William Hart did not live here. He lived ten minutes away in Norfolk, Virginia. Shortly after Jason and I moved in, Augustine's daughter moved into her own apartment, and one of her sons also moved out.

There were five of us that lived there. With many mouths to feed, I wondered how this was going to be possible. Theo was the only person working. He had a job delivering newspapers to Ida Barbour residents. He had the job for about a month at the time. One day after school and within a month of moving in, Augustine said Jason and I had to learn the paper route. She also said that we would earn an allowance every Friday. I was mad. This meant after walking four miles Monday through Friday, I had to come home daily and deliver newspapers.

One rainy day after school, Theo, Jason, and I placed the newspapers into plastic bags, loaded them into our grocery carts and we all walked off. As he taught us our routes, we learned that I would manage one end of Ida Barbour and Jason the other. I felt like a fool pushing a grocery cart filled with newspapers through the projects. This continued daily until it was Friday. After completing our paper route, we were given ten dollars. That Saturday morning, Augustine woke us up around 4:00 a.m. The newspapers were delivered to our front door. Jason, Theo, and I would drag them into the house. Then Jason and I would rubber band the newspapers, count the amount we needed, and loaded our carts. Once the sun rose, Jason and I left the house. After I finished, I walked to the barbershop and had my name (Curt) cut along the back of my head. The following Friday, we received another ten dollars, and I spent it at the candy lady's house.

By my third week, I delivered newspapers by myself. My route took me two hours or more to complete. Often I would miss an apartment or two and would have to walk back out to deliver it. While physically exhausted, it was Friday and I looked forward to the ten dollars. However, Jason and I did not receive an allowance this week. We were pissed. Additionally, Theo stopped delivering newspapers and they both kept the money. Jason and I began to sell our extra newspapers and keep the money for ourselves.

School was tolerable. I was enrolled into all accelerated classes. My classmates were smart. Often we would do dumb things to disrupt class. However, when we disrupted Coach Toad's science class, he would walk us outside the classroom, talk to us and we would straighten up. Coach Toad was a veteran and although he was cool, he was also very intimidating in that he was tall and had broad shoulders. Every morning when we entered his classroom, and asked him, "How was he doing that morning?" In a deep baritone voice, his response was always the same, "GOOD!" Although he often had to walk me outside of his classroom, I did appreciate him not sending me to the office. Because I was grieving along with physical and mental exhaustion, my grades declined. I began to care less about school and more about getting rest.

December 25, 1988, was our first Christmas without our mom. That morning, Jason and I walked downstairs, and someone said, "Merry Christmas." We replied with "Merry Christmas." I was not expecting anything and was surprised when I was handed two boxes. Augustine had bought me and Jason a winter jacket and a pair of grayish black stonewash jeans with Velcro pockets on each side. We were grateful.

At school, somehow I was able to improve my grades. When report cards were handed out, I was happy that I had earned honor roll status again. As I walked home, there was a lady sitting on her porch that I delivered newspapers to. She asked me how I was doing, and I said fine. I shared my academic achievement with her, and she was happy for me. She also said that she could not wait to speak with my Aunt Augustine about it. That evening after my paper route, I was standing in the front room looking out the front door, when Augustine approached me with a frown on her face and said, "Do not tell anyone you made the honor roll!" and angrily walked away. I could not believe what I had just heard. It was at that point that I knew that she was not rooting for us to succeed.

For the remainder of the year, my grades were up and down. A few days before school ended, I was in my English class preparing to take a test that counted more towards our final grade than usual. My teacher's name was Mr. Manny, and he knew that I had a D average. He had already told me that if I failed the exam, I would fail English. I do not remember exactly at what point of time this happened in class, but Mr. Manny made it known to my classmates that I needed to pass the exam to pass his class. He also made it known to me that they all were rooting for me to succeed. Once I completed my exam, I walked towards his desk and placed the paper face down on the table. I was nervous. Once he graded my exam and calculated my average, he made an announcement to the class that I passed. As everyone clapped and cheered, tears fell from my eyes. I thanked and appreciated them all.

CHAPTER 6

Summer of June 1989

We were happy when school ended. Unfortunately, we spent the summer delivering newspapers and doing chores. Our chores consisted of sweeping, mopping, cleaning toilets, dusting, and ironing everyone's clothes. I can remember counting and ironing at least fifty garments on one Saturday that summer.

Often, Uncle William would visit us. He would walk through the front door smiling like he had won the lottery. He was dark skinned, stood five feet ten inches, had a gold tooth and a mini-Afro. He also drove a nice maroon Cadillac and always dressed like he had just returned from church. He knew he looked good, and it was good to see him; however, when Augustine entered the living room, the atmosphere became toxic. She always spoke to him in a nasty tone. He would reply, and a few moments later he would leave. But before doing so, he would give Jason and I a couple of dollars. We thanked him and asked him if we could stay with him every other weekend. He said yes and kept his word.

That same summer, I was at home looking out of our back door when I saw someone that looked familiar. It was a guy named "Blowpop" that I knew from JDUB. I was so happy to see someone from my old neighborhood. As he walked up, I cracked the screen door and said, "Hello." He said, "Man you look like Godzilla, I did not know who you were." As I laughed it off, I knew that he said that because I had a lot of acne. We spoke briefly and then he continued walking wherever he was going. Later that day, I saw a good friend walking down the street. His name was Jamal. He was a slim, brown skinned brother, and one of the most popular guys out the Ida Barbour. When we had a chance, we enjoyed playing basketball, video games, wrestling each other and talking to girls. However, there was nothing we loved more than cracking jokes on each other.

CHAPTER 7

My Sophomore School Year

September 1989, summer ended, and it was time to start my sophomore year of high school. Unfortunately, Jason and I did not have one new item to wear. Everything we had was worn out. When the alarm sounded, I would get dressed. Either Augustine cooked me a grilled cheese sandwich or ate some Corn Flakes with sugar. As I ate in the front room, Augustine played the radio every morning and that was a relief; because I did not want to hear anything she had to say. The radio stationed played "Jesus is Lord" by The Commodores every morning. Even though I enjoyed the song, my challenges made it difficult to believe the lyrics. Upon returning to school, it was great seeing and talking to my friends. But it was difficult looking like a bum. I had Marine Corps Junior Reserve Officers Training Corps (JROTC) as a course. The course taught me how to: march, conduct physical training, recognize military rank, conduct drill and ceremony, and rappel. While I did find these tasks interesting, the course addressed one of my biggest concerns, which was the need for clothing.

Jason and I faced the same challenges again this school year. My grades were up and down. Participating in after school activities was not an option, and neither was attending the high school basketball and football games. On top of that, Augustine never tried to take us to visit our grandmother, and regrettably, in October of 1989, she passed away. Although I do not remember much, we did attend her funeral. I believed that she died from a broken heart because she was lonely and missed her family.

Every Wednesday, I had to wear my JROTC uniform to school. One day I decided to walk through Ida Barbour instead of quickly exiting the park. I had never done this before, so as I walked through the park, I was extremely cautious of my surroundings. As I walked closer to where I could exit, I noticed that there was a man standing close by, and as I walked towards him, he spoke and began to walk towards me. When I tried to walk past him, he pulled out a gun, pointed it at me, and asked for my money. I gave him everything in my pockets. He then forced me to walk with him to an apartment where he knocked on the back door and a guy opened it. I quickly realize that he was there to buy drugs and that is exactly what he did. Afterwards, he walked me back to where he had pulled the gun on me and told me that if I had not given him my money, he would have shot me, but not with the intent of killing me.

After an ordeal like this, the average child would have gone home, but I continued to London Oaks and caught the bus to school. After school, I never said anything to Augustine about what had transpired that day.

After I finished my paper route, I told Jamal what I had experienced. He asked me, "If I had said anything to Augustine," and I said "No!" He then asked me, "If I knew what the guy looked like," and I said, "Yes." Jamal replied that, "Whenever we see him, we are going to fu$$ him up on site." A few days later, Jamal and I were standing outside our front door when I saw the crackhead walking down the street. Jamal looked at me and asked me, "What did I want to do?" I said, "To let it go because Jason and I had to walk those streets every day, and we did not need any more problems." I never walked through the park again.

CHAPTER 8

The Politician / The Police Officers / The Attorney

I do not remember much about Jason's experiences in school; however, I do remember being relieved that he had friends, and that no one picked on him because he did not have enough school clothes. I can recall on one day after school, Jason telling me that he had met a man at school, that I believe was a politician that was running for office named Mr. Patterson. Jason had also met a Portsmouth police officer named Detective Viviana Black, who talked to him about the Junior Police Explorer's program they offered. Jason encouraged me to meet Detective Black and at some point I did. She was a nice lady, and since Jason trusted her I considered joining the program. We asked Augustine if we could join and surprisingly, she gave us her consent.

Once a week we had our Junior Police Explorer meetings. We had to put on our Junior Police Explorers uniforms and walk a mile and a half to the Portsmouth Police Station after we delivered our newspapers. I must admit that it felt uncomfortable walking through Ida

Barbour with that uniform on, but no one bothered us. During the meetings, we discussed upcoming events and considered ways to recruit new explorers and improve the program. After the meetings, we rode home in the police car. When we stepped out of the car people stared but no one ever said anything to us.

Later during my sophomore year, Augustine told Jason and me that our mother had left us a life insurance policy. Augustine also said that "She was the custodian of the policy and that when I turned eighteen, she would have to sign the paperwork over to me so that I could receive the money." I was already aware of this, so I just said, "OKAY." Augustine went on expressing how the food stamps she received for Jason and me were not enough. So, she told Jason and me to put on our worst clothes, which we found easy to do. My only pair of sneakers had a gaping hole in the soles, and to keep my feet from getting wet, I tucked my socks underneath my feet. We walked outside, got in the back seat of my cousin's car, and rode downtown to a Portsmouth bank. While my cousin sat outside, Augustine, Jason and I walked inside. As we sat and waited, we were greeted by a man named Mr. Peoples. We all rode the elevator up to his office where he explained his role as the attorney responsible for managing our life insurance policy. Then Mr. Peoples inquired as to how he could help us. Augustine began to explain that the amount of food stamps she received was not enough to provide food for us. Mr. Peoples said that he understood and was willing to help. At the end of the meeting, he gave each of us his business card, thanked us for stopping by and said he would be in touch.

Later that night, Jason and I discussed our visit with the attorney. We knew Augustine was lying. So, the next day, I called Mr. Peoples from school and told him that she was lying. Augustine received enough to feed Jason and I. She wanted more food stamps to feed herself and her two grown sons. I told him that she did not need anything else for us. He thanked me and Augustine never received anything extra.

On December 25, 1989, again Jason and I did not expect to receive anything for Christmas, but we were grateful that we received a pair of pants and a shirt. A couple of months later, we moved out of Ida Barbour and into a two-bedroom, one bath house on London Blvd. This was a much closer walk to the London Oaks bus stop for me. But unfortunately, we now lived a mile from Ida Barbour and Augustine wanted to keep the newspaper route. We would now have to walk an extra mile across two busy highways before we could place our first newspaper inside someone's screen door. Reluctantly, Jason and I continued to deliver our newspapers using a grocery cart through all kinds of weather for free.

We also continued to take part in the Junior Police Explorers Program. Detective Black began picking us up, and after our meeting, she drove us back home.

The end of my sophomore year was near. My tenth-grade English teacher's name was Ms. Paxton, and she was a nice lady. I had to write a term paper and had a week to do so. When my paper was due, I did not turn it in. I never worked on it. After class Ms. Paxton talked with me. She said that "If I did not turn it in, I would fail." So, she was kind enough to extend me three more days. I thanked her. After school, I walked home and delivered newspapers. I knew I had to complete my term paper, but I was too tired and lacked the desire, plus I thought more about the upcoming summer. On the day it was due, I did not turn it in. My teacher was disappointed in me and had no choice but to fail me. Augustine never asked me about it.

CHAPTER 9

Summer of June 1990

My high school had a program that helped students obtain summer jobs, and I was able to get a job working for the Portsmouth Parks & Recreation. It worked Monday through Friday from 8:30 a.m. to 4:30 p.m. I was happy and looked forward to receiving my first paycheck. I could get my ear pierced, buy a herringbone gold chain, and new school clothes. I could also help my brother and the possibility of being able to do all of this sounded great.

Early Monday morning, I walked from London Blvd to the Portsmouth Public Library where I met the work crew. I spent my day riding in a truck and cleaning all over the city. At lunchtime, I sat and ate with the guys. They were a cool group and I had fun. After work, they drove me home and I continued delivering newspapers. On the weekends after delivering newspapers and completing my chores, I rode Theo's bike from London Blvd to Jeffrey Wilson, and with no oversight, I did what I wanted. I played basketball, met with friends to play video games, and visited my family. I also saw Moo and Big Orange who were like big brothers to me. When my mother was alive, I would walk to their apartment, and we would toss the football or baseball back and forth. We also played

Spades and Tunk. As I spoke with Moo, he spoke about a summer basketball league that he was coaching, and asked me, "If I wanted to play?" Not knowing exactly how I would be able to do this, I reluctantly said, "Yes." I then rode off and returned home. Once I returned Theo's bike, I walked to Ida Barbour to link up with Jamal and others. We would roam throughout Ida Barbour joking and wrestling. There would always be a group of older guys we knew. We asked them to buy us alcohol and they did. After drinking the alcohol, I would stagger home, walked straight into our bedroom, and pass out.

After I delivered newspapers on Sunday, I told Augustine I wanted to attend Reverend Steel's church on Turnpike Road. She said that it was fine, but that day, I never made it to church. I walked to the Mount Herman Gym and met up with Coach Moo. Happy to see me, Coach Moo handed me my jersey. Running frantically to the locker room, I changed my clothes and warmed up with our team. Before the game began, I checked in at the scorer's table. The man asked me my name, and I said Curtis Hicks. Even though we lost that game by one point, I lead our team in scoring with fifteen points. That same day, there was a second game. This time, I walked to the table and said my name was Tony Hicks. We won that game! I was not the leading scorer, but I scored seventeen points. Afterwards, I changed my clothes, talked to my friends, and walked back home.

Every Wednesday, the local newspaper published something they called "The Currents." It showed the scores of local sports teams. Augustine enjoyed sports and she always read "The Currents." She had no idea I was playing. Since I had two good games, my name could make the paper. So, I talked to Jason. On Wednesday, I suggested that we carry every newspaper out of the house. That way we could check to see if I was mentioned, and Jason agreed. When we checked, there was no mention of me. However, the following

Wednesday, they ran an article that mentioned both Curtis Hicks and Tony Hicks. After Jason completed his route, he returned home with no newspapers, and when I finished my route, I had an extra five newspapers. So, on my way home, I opened each paper and trashed "The Currents" section. Later that evening, Augustine complained and asked me if I knew why our newspapers did not contain "The Currents" section? I said, "I did not know," and walked into our bedroom.

> ATLANTIC COAST 46, MELVIN & BULLOCK 45 — led the winners with 22. Tony Hicks bucketed 17 for M&B.

> MELVIN & Bullock 54, CULPEPPER RADIATOR 53 — racked up 20 for M&B. Curtis Hicks added 15. For Culpepper scored 28.

The next morning, I walked to work and afterwards I completed my paper route. By this time, Jason fully trusted Mr. Patterson (the politician) and often stated that he was a good man. I cannot remember exactly why Jason suggested we call him on this day, but after we finished our paper routes, Jason and I walked to a pay phone and called him. He agreed to come and meet us. This was my first time meeting him. However, Jason told me he was a White, middle aged man. When he arrived, we all sat in his car and talked. He listened to our concerns which had a lot to do with our living conditions. We also explained why we did not want Augustine to know about him and he understood. Mr. Patterson bought us food to eat, gave us money and told us that, "If we ever needed money for food or clothing, let him know." We thanked him and we all departed.

I continued to enjoy my job. Before I could get paid, I had to work a week in the hold. This meant I would have to work three full weeks before I earned my first check. After that, my paydays would occur every two weeks. That Friday, my first paycheck was two hundred and fifteen dollars. I was so excited. Augustine knew it was payday too. When I got home from work, she asked me if I wanted her to cash my check. Since I did not have a way to cash it, I said, "OKAY." The next morning, Augustine walked into the front room and handed me fifteen dollars. She told me to buy my pens, pencils, and notebooks for school. She kept the rest of my money, and I was furious. I began to experience a wide range of emotions with anger and frustration being at the root of my emotions. First, some of the people who knew my mother had stolen her personal belongings and now Augustine was doing the same thing to me. I felt like I was working for nothing yet again.

One Wednesday night, Augustine asked something of me, and I snapped. I put up my fists and dared her to come near me. When her son stepped towards me, I walked into our room with tears of anger falling from my eyes. That night I told Jason I was not giving her my money again. I also told him I was planning to leave. That following Thursday night, I packed my clothes and sat them outside the house, and on Friday morning, I told my brother I was sorry, but I had to go. I also told him to hang in there, and I walked out of the house, grabbed my bag, and walked to work. After work, I cashed my check and walked to Jeffrey Wilson. I visited my family and told them what it was like living with Augustine. It led to me sleeping several nights at their house.

The following week, I decided to not go back to work, and since it was the summertime, I woke up and played with my friends out JDUB. Although it was my decision to leave Augustine's house, I really worried about Jason. Since we did not have a house phone, the only way I could communicate with Jason was to catch him during his evening paper route. So, I borrowed a bike and rode it from the JDUB to Ida Barbour to look for him. I rode around until I saw him, and when I finally saw him, we were so happy to see each other. I made sure he was ok and had a few dollars. Then we scheduled for the next time we would meet up. We encouraged each other to remain strong, and then I rode back to JDUB.

For the next three weeks, I done whatever I wanted to do. One weekend, Midnight, Steve, and I walked from JDUB to Ida Barbour. They met my friends, and we all spent time together until around 1:00 a.m. We began to walk back to JDUB. At the corner of County Street and Turnpike Road, there was a gas station and car dealership nearby. While we were walking by the car dealership, a police car saw us walking. The officer cut on his lights and drove over to where we stood. The police officer asked us where we were coming from, and we told him. Then he asked us if we were stealing cars and we said no. The police officer told us to get in his car and he drove us back to JDUB.

When I ran out of money and wore out my welcome from living with family, I turned to friends out JDUB and asked if I could spend the night with them. They allowed me too. And while I was grateful, every morning, I woke up hungry because I had nothing to eat. So, I linked up with a guy out JDUB and started selling crack rock.

CHAPTER 10

Legal Guardians

Before I walked out of Augustine's house, Jason and I never missed a Police Explorer's meeting. When I did not show up for our meetings, Detective Black asked Jason about me, and he told her what was going on. That day, Detective Black and Jason drove to the JDUB to pick me up. We all sat down and talked. Afterwards, Detective Black wanted to help us, so she drove us to Augustine's house. While Jason and I remained in the police car, Detective Black walked to the door and asked to speak with Augustine. When their conversation was over, Jason and I walked into the house, grabbed our belongings, and walked out. That night we stayed with Detective Black, her husband Sergeant Black, and her son Jasper. The next morning, Detective Black asked us if we wanted to live with them and we agreed.

In August of 1990, with just two weeks before I started my junior year of high school, they became our legal guardians. This was a blessing. We now lived in a large house in a quiet neighborhood in the Parkview Community in Portsmouth. I had my own room while Jason and Jasper shared a room. Since school was about to start, Detective Black took us to the mall and bought us whatever we needed. We were grateful. Once school started, Detective Black drove me to school every day. But one morning as I walked outside to get into the police car, I met her dad. He was a nice easy-going man, and he began to drive me to school every day. He was always on time, and I really enjoyed talking to him. Since our guardians worked, after school I caught the bus to London Oaks. From there, I walked home. It was a twenty-minute walk. A week later, Jason and I visited Detective Black's parents. They lived in a community called Cavalier Manor. Her parents were nice people. While I enjoyed the visit, as I sat on their front porch, I realized that I missed my friends. I also really missed my mom, my grandmother, Uncle William, and Aunt Lauren who had all passed away.

I started to enjoy school a little more, and now that my friends knew that I lived with police officers, they often made jokes. It was cool and I always joked back. One evening at our Police Explorer's meeting, we were brainstorming ideas to promote our program. Detective Black suggested that we wear our Police Explorer's uniform to school. Even though I felt like it was a bad idea, I agreed. The next morning, on my way to school, I thought about my friends. They did not know about our Police Explorer's Program. When I stepped out of the car, I had everyone's attention. From that point on, it was joke after joke after joke. When my first period class began, my friends joked. In second period, we disrupted class so much that the teacher sent me to the office and requested that I be sent home. The mission was not a complete failure because three of my good friends from an area of Portsmouth called Churchland (Reginald, Grady, Kyle) joined our program.

A few weeks later, I was sitting in my homeroom class, when over the loud speak, an administrator made an announcement regarding our homecoming and began naming students that were involved. As I listened, I realized that the students that were named were high academic achievers. Moments later, I heard my name called. I was surprised and I knew they made a mistake. As I walked to the office to address the error, I talked to a teacher in the hallway. She was so happy for me and said that the teachers had voted for me to take part in our homecoming. They recognized the path that I was on academically prior to my mother's death and considered it. I brought the news home to Detective and Sergeant Black, and they were happy for me. On the night of our homecoming, I wore a nice black and white tuxedo. I looked and felt great. My escort was an incredibly quiet and bright girl. During the ceremony, she never said a word and barely looked at me. In school, she did not say much to anyone, so it did not bother me. Once I heard my name called in front of the crowd, it was all good. My picture was in the local paper, and I was happy.

Homecoming Escort

Curtis Hicks

Later that school year, I signed up to take the Armed Services Vocational Aptitude Battery test (ASVAB). I done so to get out of class. Two weeks later, on a Saturday morning, someone rang our doorbell. Detective Black opened the door and called me downstairs. When I opened the door, it was the recruiters from the United States Marine Corps. They were there to talk to me about joining the Corps. I told them that I was not interested and closed the door. Throughout the week, they started calling our house. I did not answer the phone, because I wanted no parts of it.

CHAPTER 11

Horsefly & Quanta

Our first Christmas with the Blacks was nice, and we received all kinds of clothes and gifts. Over the Christmas break we traveled three hours to a nice resort in New Bern, North Carolina, and we also visited Detective Black's family in Columbia, Maryland. They were all nice, they treated us well and we had fun. Even though our conditions had improved, I found it difficult to feel good. I missed my mom and my family. After the holidays, we returned to school. It was now January 1991, and in my homeroom class, I became friends with a guy we called Horsefly. He was a cool guy. We were always joking around, and our thoughts were always about girls and sports. One Saturday, we had to attend school for a makeup snow day. Horsefly and I did not want to be there, so he suggested skipping a class. Even though I was nervous, I agreed. When class began we hung out in the male bathroom passing time. We attended the rest of our classes and the school day ended.

One day, the school administrator made an announcement for me to report to the office. As I strolled through the hallways looking into every class, I saw a very pretty girl. I continued to the office and circled back afterwards. I walked past her classroom, and I saw her again. The very next day, I walked out of my sixth period class, and as I stood in the hallway, I saw the same girl walk out of a classroom. She did not notice me, but I stared and smiled. A few moments later, a friend of mine named Ricky walked out of the same classroom, so I asked him about her. He said, "Her name was Quanta, and she did not have a boyfriend." I asked him "To mention me to her to see if she was interested." and he said, "OKAY."

The next morning, I walked through the hallways before going to homeroom, and I saw Rocky talking to Quanta. When he pointed in my direction, I smiled and continued to homeroom. At the end of the day, as the students exited their classrooms, I slowly walked and stood in the hallway. I waited to see Quanta. As she walked by, she looked at me, smiled, and said, "Hi." I smiled and spoke. Ricky walked up to me and handed me a piece of paper with Quanta's phone number on it. I called her when I got home, and it was on. Quanta was a first-year student in high school, and she lived with her mom out in Churchland. Before class, Quanta and I talked, and every time I saw her, she looked pretty. On the weekends, I wanted to hang out with her. So, I asked Detective Black and Quanta asked her mother named Ms. Janet if we could see each other. They agreed that I could only visit Quanta if Ms. Janet was home.

One Saturday afternoon, I caught the city bus to Churchland and walked to Quanta's house. We hung out for a couple of hours. Afterwards, Ms. Janet cooked for me and gave me a ride home. When Ms. Janet and Quanta dropped me off, they met my guardians and my brothers. It was a good day, and this continued in the weekends to come. While this was great, I wanted to spend more time with Quanta. Especially when her mom was not around. So, after school, I began riding the school bus to her house instead of going straight home. This continued for a while until one day, someone knocked on the door. Quanta looked out her window and saw a police officer. It was Sergeant Black. When I opened the door, he began fussing at me. He told me to get into the car and he drove me home. Afterwards, Sergeant Black told me a Portsmouth police officer who lived across the street from Quanta had been watching me get off Quanta's school bus every day. I had no idea that police officer knew my guardians. Sergeant Black told me to come straight home from school and I complied. However, that did not last long because I began going back to Quanta house after school.

One morning before school, Horsefly and I met in the school parking lot. We talked and decided we were going to skip the entire day. That morning we walked to someone's house Horsefly knew out in Old Churchland. We all sat down, talked, and watched television. The guy was much older than us. He said that "If we had money and wanted beer, he would buy it." We said, "OKAY." At 9:30 a.m., we walked to the Seven Eleven and he bought us a six pack of Blue Bulls in the can. We walked back to his house, and I quickly drunk three on an empty stomach. Once the beer was gone, I was ready to go. As we walked, I told Horsefly that I was hungry. At school, it was close to our lunchtime. So, we walked there and two minutes after we arrived the bell rang. I staggered to our cafeteria and ate everything in sight. After lunch, for some crazy reason, I decided to stay in school. So, I staggered to my class and took my seat. Moments later, my head began to spin. The teacher knew something was wrong with me, so she sent me to the nurse's office. When I sat down in the nurse's office, I was so drunk that I could barely sit upright. As I waited to be seen, I vomited in the office. It was disgusting and I was embarrassed; however, that was the least of my concerns. The school called Detective Black and she was upset. She put me on punishment, and I could not leave the house.

I continued to skip school and done what I wanted to do. One day, Horsefly and I skipped school. As we walked to old Churchland, he said that "He had a stolen car," and he walked me to it. When I sat on the passenger's side, I noticed the car's ignition switch had been removed. Horsefly knew how to start the car using a screw-driver. But before we drove it, we walked a couple of blocks, removed the license plates off another car and put them on the stolen car. Then, I told him that I wanted to drive to Conway, North Carolina to visit my family. My mother had driven me there so many times that I knew exactly how to get back. Although this was my first-time driving, I drove over an hour to my Aunt Mary's house, and it was great to see her again. After an hour or so, I drove off and we stopped at the local gas station in Conway. I walked in and Aunt Mary's husband was in there talking. I spoke and paid for our gas, and then I drove back to Portsmouth where we dumped the car.

At school, my grades were average, because I did not put any effort into my studies. After school, I continued to go to Quanta's house, and there were times when I had bus fare to get home and other times that I did not. If I did not, I would ask my friends that lived in Churchland for a ride. While some drove me home, others said no. Once I wore out my welcome with car rides, I had another idea of how I could get home. One evening, I used a payphone in Old Churchland to call a taxi. When the driver arrived and asked me where I was going? I said, "Sir I am going to Jeffrey Wilson. I do not have the money on me. If it is OKAY, my aunt will pay you when we get there." As I stood there wearing my JROTC uniform, he said, "That was fine." He drove off and we conversed. I was nice and respectful the entire time. When we arrived, I would ask him to hold on as I opened the car door, and walked to someone's apartment that I did not know. Gently knocking, the intent was for no one to hear me, and they did not. Seconds later, I would turn around and put my index finger up signally to the driver to wait a minute. I would walk towards the back of the building as if I were going to knock on the back door and run off. Afterwards, I would then walk from JDUB to Parkview.

I done this quite often and managed to not get caught. However, I got tired of walking from JDUB to Parkview. So, this time I called a taxi from Churchland and asked him to take me to Parkview. Once we entered Parkview, I had the taxi driver drop me off four blocks from where I lived. As soon as the car stopped, I opened the door and immediately ran off. Zigzagging between houses, I made it home and I thought that I had escaped but I was wrong. A few moments later, Detective Black walked into the house and asked me to come outside. I walked out on to the porch and the taxi driver said, "Yes that's him." Detective Black paid the driver and she fussed at me.

A couple of weeks later, Horsefly and I decided to skip school again and caught the city bus to the mall. Afterwards, I asked him, "If he wanted to come to my house?," and he said, "OKAY." When we walked into the house, I began to show him around. Then we walked to our kitchen and out the back door. Within minutes, the home alarm beeped suggesting someone had opened the front door. It was Detective Black. She walked out the back door, asked for my house key, and told us to leave. I walked Horsefly to the city bus stop, and he rode it home. I turned around and walked back home and noticed that there was a police car parked in front of our house. That meant someone was home, so I rang the doorbell and there was no response. I knocked on the door and still no one answered. With nowhere to go, I walked off and wandered around for two hours before returning home. I rang the doorbell, and again no one answered! Since it was getting dark, I had to do something. So, I walked to Ida Barbour and spent all night walking throughout the park. Early the next morning, I walked back to the house. I knew that Jason and Jasper would be getting ready for school. So, I rang the doorbell and Detective Black opened the door. She told me to get my book bag and wait on the porch until her dad arrived. I could not shower, change clothes, or brush my teeth. When I arrived at school, I told Horsefly that I was skipping school that day, and he skipped with me. After school, I caught the London Oaks' bus and walked straight home. When I rang the doorbell, Detective Black opened the door and this time she let me in. She said our neighbors had been watching the house and saw me bring a guy into her house. She also said I was restricted to the house until further notice. The following Saturday, Sergeant Black had to work. It was a nice day, and it was killing me to be in the house. So that afternoon, I told Jason that "I could not live there anymore, and I was leaving." Jason looked at me confused and asked, "Where I would go?" I said I did not know, but on this day in March of 1991, a few months before the end of my junior year, I packed my bags and walked out.

CHAPTER 12

Ms. Bridget Marie Martinez / Ida Barbour

Feeling down and out, and not knowing where I was going, my first stop was Ida Barbour. I walked there and the first person I saw was Jamal, I told him that I had walked out of Detective Black's house, and that I would not be living there anymore. He said that "He was sorry to hear that, and he wanted to help me." Jamal walked into his apartment and spoke with his mom. She then called me into her apartment, and we talked. Afterwards, she made a phone call and Jamal walked with me to meet his aunt, Ms. Martinez, and her son Stephen. They lived down the other end of the Ida Barbour near the rental office. When we lived in Ida Barbour, Jason delivered newspapers down this end. Therefore, I had never seen them before. I walked into her apartment, introduced myself, and we talked. After our conversation, Ms. Martinez said I could spend the night there and I agreed. The next day, Ms. Martinez called Detective Black and they talked. It was decided that I would begin living with Ms. Martinez and her son.

Ms. Martinez was a nice lady and very pleasant to everyone. It seemed like everyone knew and liked her. I never heard her curse or raise her voice. When children were around, they loved her, and she loved them back. Stephen was cool and much younger than I was, but I could tell he was a good son. Like Detective Black, Ms. Martinez treated me like her own son, and although I felt like I was living with the right person, I did not understand why Ms. Martinez would do this for me. She did not know much about me, and it did not matter. She saw that I was a confused child that needed a place to live, and she wanted to help. She showed that she cared, and this humbled me, and I began to change my life for the better.

Early Monday morning, I heard Ms. Martinez saying, "Curt it is time to wake up." I responded with "Yes Ma'am," cleaned myself up, ate breakfast, and once again I began to walk back to my old bus stop in London Oaks. This time, I didn't mind the walk because it gave me time to think and clear my head. I spent a lot of time thinking about my brother, Aunt Mary and her husband, Augustine, and all my family members who were now deceased. I also thought about Detective and Sergeant Black and how I really did not appreciate them and what they were trying to do for us. This was a hard reality and another reason for me to focus on changing my behavior.

After school, I walked home, done my homework, and ate dinner. I would also call Jason to see how he was doing. I missed my brother; but I knew he was with good people, and this gave me peace of mind. Later that week, I met Stephen's dad Mr. Eli. He was a big muscular man who stood well over six feet tall. He had served in The Marines, and although I was a little scared of him, we bonded together well. He began driving me to the London Oaks' bus stop every morning. After school, I caught the bus back to London Oaks and walked home. On Saturday when I went to Quanta's house, Ms. Janet would drive me home. This time I introduced them to Ms. Martinez and Stephen. On Sunday, I attended church with Ms. Martinez, which was the same church that Jamal and his family attended. Several Sunday's later, someone asked Jamal and I to consider singing a song for the congregation. The song was "Tomorrow" by The Winans. We agreed and began to practice. When we performed the elders loved it. Jamal could really sing.

I was about to complete my junior year of high school and it was the last week of school. Although I was classified as a junior, I had been taking tenth grade English. I really wanted to attend summer school and complete eleventh grade English so that I would be back on track to graduate with my class, but I did not have the money. So, instead of allowing me to waste my summer, Ms. Martinez helped me get a job working at McDonald's at the Portsmouth Naval Hospital. I was thankful. I had to walk a mile to and from work, and I worked three or four days a week. On Sundays, I volunteered to work from noon until midnight. When my shift was over, my manager gave me a ride home. On payday, Quanta's mother drove us to the movies. A few weeks before school started, I bought my school clothes, and all the while I was working, Ms. Martinez never asked me for a dime. I was happy with the way things were going.

CHAPTER 13

Twelfth Grade Year

I began my senior year in high school in September of 1991. It was Quanta's sophomore year and the city had built us a *new* high school that was nice. I appreciated Mr. Eli for continuing to take me to the bus stop every morning. At school, my class schedule was easy and that was exactly how I wanted it. I was determined to do just enough to pass; because my main goal was to earn money, so I needed to work.

This year was no different from the past years in that Horsefly and I continued to skip school. We still caught the city bus to the mall and played video games. One morning, as we walked through the student parking lot, Horsefly saw a friend of his and asked for a ride to old Churchland. Horsefly then walked me to a stolen car and told me that, "I could drive it, but I had to avoid the area near our new high school. I said, "OKAY," but I did not listen. When our school day ended, I drove to our high school and picked up Quanta. When she got into the car, she asked me "Whose car I was driving?" I do not remember what I told her. However, I drove off and stopped at a red light at the corner of Cedar Lane and West Norfolk Road. Then, I made a right onto West Norfolk Road. The road was narrow with large trees on each side. As I looked ahead, I said, "Oh sh$$!" Quanta asked, "What was wrong?" I told her "The car was stolen, and the police were stopping traffic ahead." While Quanta was mad, I had to do something quick to keep us from getting caught. There were about eight cars ahead of us, so as I slowly drove closer, I looked to the left, and I saw a narrow entrance into someone's driveway. I quickly pulled into the driveway, slowly backed out as if we lived there and drove in the opposite direction. My heart was pounding, and I hoped that the police did not notice. Fortunately for us, they did not. I drove Quanta home, parked away from her building, and we walked into her apartment. An hour later, Quanta heard some commotion coming from outside, and when she looked out the window, she said it was the police. They had found the stolen car and were having it towed away. I was relieved.

On the weekends that I visited Quanta, after our visits, I walked to Horscfly's house. One night, we decided to walk to the grocery store. We stole two bottles of the larger bottles of Wild Irish Rose. Drinking as we walked, we finally made it back to his house where we played cards for quarters. I started talking about getting my left ear pierced and he said that he could do it. At first, I was hesitant, but since I was drunk, I said, "OKAY!" So, he gave me a couple of ice cubes and a paper towel to numb my ear, while he cleaned an extra earring with rubbing alcohol. A few moments later, he pushed it through my left ear lobe, and it made a nasty popping sound. I thoroughly cleaned my ear by applying rubbing alcohol. Afterwards, I fastened the back of the earring. For the next two weeks, I cleaned my ear daily, and I never had a problem with my ear.

Two weeks before the end of the school year, I had missed twenty-nine days of school and thirty days was the max, and I still had not completed my twelfth-grade English class. High school graduation was held during the last week in May of 1992. This was an exciting time for everyone but me. As my friends walked across the stage, I was a little disappointed that I was not walking with them. However, that summer, Ms. Martinez helped me enroll into night school. I was glad that she did not allow me to drag my feet, and that Mr. Eli was willing to give me a ride to night school. Eventually, a met a guy at night school and I paid him to drive me home afterwards. I finally completed night school and earned my high school diploma in January of 1993.

High School Diploma

CHAPTER 14

Insurance Policy

After receiving my diploma, I did not have any plans and I was not interested in college. So, I continued to work at McDonald's, but on this one day, I thought about my mom's life insurance policy. I realized that if I ever wanted what was mines that I would have to speak to Augustine. Of course, this was something that I did not want to do. So, I spoke with Ms. Martinez, and she suggested that I reach out to our attorney Mr. Peoples. I contacted his office at the downtown Portsmouth bank and scheduled a meeting. Mr. Peoples informed me that my mom had a thirty-thousand-dollar life insurance policy. He also told me that if Augustine signed it over, I would receive half of that amount and that he would contact Augustine. A few days later, Mr. Peoples call to say that after speaking with Augustine, "The only way that she would sign over the policy was if I were to give her nine hundred dollars of my portion of the money." I agreed and later that week, Augustine's son met me at the bank. We barely spoke or looked at each other. I gave him the money and after we parted, I felt like I had hit the lottery. I also started to live like it. I quit my job at McDonald's although I had been working there for over a year and a half and I had a great working relationship with everyone. Ms. Martinez recommended that I did not quit my job; however, she allowed me to figure things out on my own. So, instead of coming home smelling like cheeseburgers, I now came home smelling like an alcoholic.

After two attempts, I passed my driver's test, and bought a 1993 gold, four door, Hyundai Excel. It was sweet. The salespeople recommended that I make a couple of payments to start establishing my credit, but I did not listen. I paid forty-five hundred dollars in cash and headed to the rim and music shop. With my new wealth, I had fun with Jamal and my friends from Jeffrey Wilson. We ate out multiple times a day, made multiple trips to fix my car system and my newly installed fog lights, drank alcohol every day, and clubbed every weekend. I also shopped and hung out with Quanta.

I slept until noon every day, and when I woke up, I was ready to hang out. I ate out and drove around with nothing to do until Quanta came home from school. She always knew when I was nearby, because she could hear me blasting KRS-One's song "Black Cop" loudly through my two twelve-inch box speakers. I had a nice sound system, and I showed it off. Later that year, I was happy that Quanta and I participated in her junior year school prom. I was able to convince Jamal to attend with one of her good friends. This was my treat of course, so he agreed, and we all had fun.

I continued to spend money as if it would never run out. I drove to Franklin, Virginia to visit my family. While I was there, I saw Aunt Patty and her daughters, and we had fun playing cards, talking trash, eating well, and drinking beer. I also visited my Aunt Mary. By this time, she was in her early seventies. However, her mind was still sharp, and she could move around very well. She was happy to see me, and I picked her brain by asking questions about my mom and dad. My mom died on her way back home. She drove off the side of a bridge near the North Carolina borderline. She also told me that my father had died when I was eleven years old. He was an alcoholic, and this is what ended his life at an early age. She then picked up the phone and called someone named Ms. Melissa who was my dad's sister. She only lived ten minutes away from Aunt Mary, so I drove over to meet her. She was so happy to see me. She showed me a picture of my dad and we looked alike. We drove back to Portsmouth, and I continued to spend money like it grew on trees. When I say we, it's because Jamal accompanied me on these trips. We went everywhere together.

In July of 1993, I was at Quanta's house, and we were having a conversation about my future. I could not continue to spend money the way I did and not have a job. She asked me if, "I had considered the military?," and I said, "Heck no!" But *I had to do something*. So, I drove to the Portsmouth recruiting station and spoke with an Air Force recruiter. That did not go well. I was qualified but I do not believe he liked me. Since I was not interested in the Navy or Marines, he walked me into the Army's office. I met the guy in charge, and I told him I was interested. He then asked me a dozen questions. Afterwards, he sat me in front of a computer, and I completed a twenty-minute test. I passed and then he began explaining the process of joining. It all sounded great, and I agreed to join. My recruiter was cool. He was a tall, fit, white guy from Pennsylvania

CHAPTER 15

Basic Training - Fort Jackson, South Carolina

A few days later, I drove back to the recruiting station, and my recruiter told me that I did not have to retake the ASVAB test. My scores were still valid since I had passed the test when I was in high school.

On July 8, 1993, at the age of nineteen, he drove me to the Military Entrance Processing Station (MEPS) at Fort Lee, Virginia. At the MEPS I saw several doctors who checked my physical health and deemed that I was physically fine and fit for military service. I then sat down with a counselor who helped me to select a career field, which was human resources. The final step was my enlistment, in which I enlisted for four years. When we returned to the recruiting station, I drove home and told Ms. Martinez that I had enlisted in the United States Army. She was happy for me; however, when I told Jason, Jamal, and a few of my other friends, they thought I was crazy. However, they were supportive. Over the next two months, I spent time with Quanta, hung out with friends, and visited family before preparing to depart for basic training.

On September 7, 1993, my recruiter drove me to Richmond, Virginia and I spent the night in a hotel. I met some other recruits. Since we felt like that would be our last night of freedom, we acted foolishly in the hotel. The next morning, a van drove us to the MEPS to sign more paperwork and to swear in. Afterwards, I boarded a Greyhound bus and took the long ride to Fort Jackson, South Carolina. When we arrived, the police officers at the gate checked our identification cards, and the bus drove us to the Fort Jackson Reception Station. This was where I met my drill sergeants. When the bus driver opened the door, a drill sergeant walked on the bus and said, "Everybody put your heads down and shut the fu$$ up." He began telling us what we were about to do, and as I kept my head down and listened, I asked myself, "What have I gotten myself into?" The first couple of days were for administrative matters such as setting up our records and signing for uniforms and military gear. Our early mornings began with physical fitness training, where the drill sergeants focused on stretching, exercising, and running. By 0645 hours, we were already in line for breakfast or chow as it was called in the Army. We ate extremely fast and there was absolutely no talking. Afterwards, I walked back to our barracks area and waited for whatever was next.

All my drill sergeants were Black, and I lived in an open bay barracks with at least fifty other male soldiers. We all walked around like we were tough, and I could feel the competitiveness between us all. We knew our physical fitness test was approaching, and this would separate the fit from the unfit. On test day, we had to do pushups and sit-ups for two minutes and complete a two-mile run. My first event was the pushup event. After forty-five seconds I was done. As the other trainees continued to push, I could not do anymore. So, I stood up and walked to the back of the line with my head down. When my peers asked how I had done, and I said fifteen, that was all they needed to know. They knew from that point on that I was no competition. The next event was the sit-up. I used the entire two minutes and done sixty-six. Drill Sergeant Morris asked, "How I had done?" I said, "Drill sergeant I did sixty-six sit-ups." He already knew that I had not done well on the push-up event, and he said, "So you can do sit-ups and not push-ups, you're a pu$$y!" It was just day four and he already did not like me. I had fifteen minutes and fifty-four seconds to complete my two-mile run, but when I crossed the finish line, the clock read twenty-two minutes. In all honesty, I had walked most of the way. I knew I was not in shape, so I put that behind me.

Mondays through Saturdays, we were awakened at 0415 hours, by bright lights, a loud horn, and drill sergeants yelling. We quickly made our beds Army style and ran downstairs for formation. We done our physical fitness training, and afterwards, we showered, shaved, and prepped for an exceptionally long day of training. One morning, I did not shave because my skin was bad, and shaving made it worse. As I stood in line for chow, Drill Sergeant Morris walked by and asked me, "If I shaved?" I said, "No, Drill Sergeant." He said I had thirty seconds to get upstairs and get back with a razor. Upon returning and in front of all the trainees waiting for chow, I stepped on top of a brick slab and stood where everyone could see me. He made me stand on one leg, dry shave, and recite repeatedly "I will never forget to shave again." Afterwards, my face felt like it was on fire.

I was not the only hardheaded trainee in our platoon. I had become friends with Private Tate from Brooklyn, New York, and Private Sammie from Philly. One afternoon, our platoon was walking through the woods to conduct bayonet training. When we arrived, Drill Sergeant Morris told us to form a circle, and then he called two trainees to the middle of the circle to fight. This only lasted for a minute, and when he called me to the middle, I won my fight. Afterwards, I looked at Drill Sergeant Morris and he had a frown on his face. He looked as if he wanted me to lose. That afternoon, he formed the platoon, and we began to walk back to our barracks. Tate, Sammie, and I were in the rear of the formation, and as trainees sang along to Army songs, we began to throw pinecones. The soldiers were getting annoyed, but they did not say anything; however, when I hit Drill Sergeant Morris with a pinecone, he snapped. He abruptly stopped the formation and angrily walked back and forth, asking, "Who threw the pinecone?" No one responded so he asked again. I did not hear anyone say a word. So, Drill Sergeant Morris marched us back and told us to stand beside our bunkbeds. He made all of us do an excessive amount of exercising to include lifting bunkbeds in cadence. I enjoyed the extra physical training because I needed it. But the others did not feel the same way. As he walked around yelling numerical cadences, Drill Sergeant Morris made his way closer to me. He looked in my direction and said something about being a pu$$y for not snitching. I continued exercising, and once a trainee began to cry, he stopped us and called me into his office. He said that "Eight trainees had told him that I done it, and he was tired of my sh$$!" He told me, Sammie, and Tate to *"Pack our bags and leave."*

As we slowly packed, we spoke amongst ourselves asking each other "Where should we go?" We dragged our bags downstairs and walked alongside the main road, where a car drove by and stopped. It was an Army captain. He asked what we were doing, and we explained. Afterwards, he told us to go back to our unit. We walked back and sat on our bunkbeds. A few moments later, the senior drill sergeant called me into their office. He told me that they were beyond tired, and that I had to cut it out. He also said, "If they were White, they would have kicked me out by now!" This opened my eyes, and I began to listen.

On Sundays, I wrote and called Quanta. Ms. Janet allowed me to call her collect. I promised to pay my bill and I did. They were also nice enough to keep my car and I appreciated it. One Sunday I called, and Quanta informed me that someone had broken into my car and stole my speaker box. She was angry, and I was too. I thought by parking my car there no one would bother it, but I was wrong. I was not surprised. The way I showed it off, I would have done the same thing to someone else.

Towards the end of basic training, we had to complete a three-day field training exercise (FTX). In preparation for this we had to pack our rucksacks and ensure that our gear properly fit. The morning of our FTX, we signed for our weapon and dummy rounds, and at 0500 hours we walked two miles to the FTX site. When we arrived, the dining facility served us hot chow inside of a small metal trailer that was under a camouflage net. Our meal consisted of *watery* eggs, bacon, sausage, grits, biscuits and gravy, pancakes with syrup, all sorts of cereal in small boxes, and orange and apple juice. The food was good.

After chow, I put on my gear, secured my M16 rifle, and prepared for training. For hours, we walked through the woods stopping along the way to conduct training. Drill Sergeant Morris taught us to keep our weapon no more than an arm's length away. That day it was hot. The heat made me tired, and I walked off without securing my weapon. Suddenly, I heard a weapon fire, and I immediately knew that it was mines. Drill Sergeant Morris had found it lying against a tree. Like a monkey, he made me jump on trees placing my arms and legs around them. I had to count one drill sergeant, two drill sergeant until I counted to five before I could let go. I done this until he was tired. Rest assured; I never made that mistake again.

For lunch and dinner, they fed us meals ready to eat (MRE). There were twelve choices, and I did not like any of them. So, I settled for the one with spaghetti. Inside the MRE was candy, crackers, a drink mix, peanut butter, and other stuff. That evening, our student platoon sergeant set up the duty roster. We all had to pull guard duty and my duty began at 0200 hours. In full gear, I laid in a trench known as a foxhole that we had dug earlier. It was three feet deep and wide enough for me to lay my entire body in. A soldier replaced me at 0400 hours. At 0430 hours, the drill sergeants woke everyone up and we all pulled security until chow time. After chow, we trained all day.

The night before we returned to the barracks, I was inside our two-man tent with my battle buddy. Since it was raining and cold, I laid on top of my poncho liner and inside my sleeping bag. I heard a drill sergeant walking around and asking who was in each tent. Subsequently, the trainees would respond. The drill sergeant continued tent to tent until he found me. It was Drill Sergeant Morris' voice. Ten minutes later, he threw a can of gas into our tent. When the gas hit my eyes and nose, I panicked and jumped up almost ripping down my side of the tent. Then I ran away attempting to avoid the smoke. As I stood in the rain, I looked back and thought about my battle buddy, I could not leave him. So, trying to avoid the smoke, I walked back to our tent. When I opened my side of the tent, my battle buddy was laying on his side with his mask properly sealed. He was fine. I felt like a fool. Drill Sergeant Morris and others laughed and loved every bit of it.

The day before graduation, we were in the barracks and Drill Sergeant Morris told us to form a line in front of his table. As we approached, he asked if we were Regular Army or National Guard? I walked up and said Regular Army, Drill Sergeant. He responded with, "If you do not change your ways, you will not amount to sh$$." Nodding my head north and south, I said, "Yes, Drill Sergeant," and walked back to my bunkbed. The next day we had a nice ceremony and I graduated. I was a happy and proud soldier.

Private Hicks

CHAPTER 16

Job Training

After basic training, since Fort Jackson was the home of my career field, I stayed local. My basic training supply sergeant drove me to my next unit to begin my job training. It was known as Advanced Individual Training (AIT). The course was five weeks long and I learned the basics about Army human resources. Monday through Friday, we done physical fitness training, ate chow, and went to class. After two weeks and with a battle buddy, soldiers were allowed to visit the post exchange store and food court. We were also allowed to go bowling and walk to the movie theater on post. The following weekend, we were allowed to go off post. A few other soldiers and I took a taxi to the local mall. I felt free for a moment and later that evening, when I returned to the barracks, my battle buddies and I walked down the street to a club called Magruder's. When I walked in, the first thing I noticed was the beer, and I bought a twenty-four ounce can of Red Bull. It was so cold, and it tasted so good that I drunk it really fast and bought another one. As I sat watching soldiers shoot pool, my head began to spin. Not realizing that my tolerance was not the same, it did not take long before I was drunk. When it was time to go, I could not walk on my own. Two soldiers put my arms around their shoulders and walked me back to the barracks. As we walked closer to our building, we could see our platoon sergeant sitting at the desk. That was when I had to walk without their support. We entered the building, I walked straight to my room, removed my shoes, and laid on my bed. I reaped alcohol, and I felt so horrible that I rolled off my bed and fell on the floor. The same soldiers helped me by taking me to the latrine and splashing cold water on my face. Afterwards, I crawled back into bed and fell asleep. I did not get out of bed until Sunday afternoon. I was thankful for those soldiers who had helped me.

We had two weeks left until graduation, when our platoon sergeant called us into the conference room to give us our assignments for our next duty station. When he called my last name and said South Korea, I frowned and shook my head, because I knew it was a one-year unaccompanied assignment. On graduation day, Jason, Jamal, and Brian picked me up. I was excited to see them, and I was also excited to drive, so I drove home. On the way home, a state trooper pulled me over for speeding. I slowed down and we eventually made it to Portsmouth. I spent the next fourteen days with Quanta, friends, Sergeant Black, and Ms. Martinez. However, one night while I was in downtown Portsmouth, I linked up with some guys that I rarely associated with. I was driving with an open beer in the car, and they were smoking weed. As I sat at a red light near an apartment complex called Churchland North, I noticed a police car at a gas station. Once I pulled off, the police officer turned on his blue lights and began to pursue us. I told the guys that the police were coming so we rolled down the windows and threw everything out into someone's grassy yard. Then I pulled over. The officer asked for my license and registration, and I gave him my driver's license and military identification card. He smelt the marijuana and told everyone to get out. There was another police officer with him. They patted us down and told us to sit on the curb. They searched my car and did not find anything. The officer then told me to take them home and for me to go straight into the house. He said that "I had too much to lose." I complied.

On the night of my flight to South Korea, there was snow everywhere. Around 2300 hours or 11:00 p.m., Jamal and Eddie rode with me to the Washington DC International Airport.

CHAPTER 17

Dongducheon, South Korea (Camp Hovey)

It was December 1994, and I was excited because I had never flown before. I flew out at 0500 hours. It was a comfortable five-hour flight to Los Angeles, California. We arrived and I had to change flights. When I boarded my second flight, there were dozens of Koreans onboard. I put on my headphones and prepared for a twelve-hour flight to Seoul, South Korea. Throughout the flight, the attendants brought us food and snacks, and I was amazed at how a plane could fly so long. When we arrived in South Korea, it was cold and snowing there as well. I walked into the airport terminal and had no clue where to go. I did not see any Americans and I felt out of place. I kept walking and saw a medium sized booth where American soldiers were working. Looking like a confused private, I asked for help, and they told me I was in the right place. That night, a few other soldiers and I spent the night in a hotel on the local economy.

The next morning, we rode a shuttle bus on post to the reception station. I signed for military gear and waited for an assignment. That afternoon, a sergeant called us into a room. She would yell a soldier's last name and the camp assigned. If she said *Yongsan*, a soldier would be happy. However, every time she called The Second Infantry Division *(2ID)*, soldiers frowned. She called my name and said 2ID Camp Hovey. I packed my bags and rode two hours to Headquarters and Headquarters Company (HHC), Second Infantry Division, Camp Hovey. We were ten minutes from North Korea. I began processing in by signing for extreme cold weather gear. Then, I rode in a military truck to my unit and met my barracks manager where he assigned me a room. I lived in what was called a Quonset hut. It resembled a small one level tub shaped building with doors at each end, and the urinals and showers were in the middle of the hut. Afterwards, he showed me where the dining facility, barbershop, and gym were.

The following morning, due to jet lag, I was tired. South Korea was sixteen hours ahead of the United States. It was January 1995, below freezing and too cold to be outside. At 0555 hours, I reported to formation for physical training. We stretched and done pushups and sit-ups outside on the concrete. Then we ran four miles. During the run, I smelled something foul. It was difficult to breathe, but I kept running. Afterwards, I learned it was air pollution. I walked back to my room to shower. Because my Quonset huts' doors did not fully close on each side, it was very cold anytime I entered the hallway to do anything. I ate chow and reported to work at 0850 hours. I lived three minutes from where I worked. I walked into the building and met my supervisor. He told me we were preparing for a field exercise that was three days away and I was not thrilled to hear that. After work, I walked to our small post exchange and bought junk food for the field. I also bought a six pack of Blue Bull beer for one dollar and eighty cents. The next day, I called Quanta collect and told her what it was like so far. She told me that Jamal had driven my car to Ms. Martinez's apartment. I said that "It was cool." For the next two days, I packed military trucks and trailers with: barbwire, mallets, pot belly stoves, weapon racks, small and medium tents, tables, shovels, chairs, generators, black boards, and miscellaneous supplies.

In South Korea, it was mandatory males served two years of military service, so I worked with South Korean soldiers that were a part of our unit. They were known as KATUSAs which meant Korean Augmentation to The United States Army. On the day of our field exercise, I hated using camouflaged face paint because it made my acne worse. We formed a convoy and drove to the site. As I rode in the back of a *HUMMV*, I looked out the window and saw some of the local people. The women were walking while balancing large items on their heads and they did not use their hands. The men worked in large rice patty fields, and if the locals were not working, they were cooking and conversating as they squat in place. Their leg strength was incredible, but what was more impressive was that everyone looked over sixty and was in excellent shape. When we arrived at the muddy field site, it took us two hours to set up everything.

I worked out of a medium tent with three small tanks parked side by side. Each tank had its hatch down. We were concealed by a large, camouflaged net. As we began to play war games, I noticed training was taken seriously. Senior enlisted soldiers and officers were busy. When they received word the full bird colonel was on his way, they stressed out even more. It was so cold that I had to wear my extreme cold weather gear. We called the puffy jacket and pants a bear suit, and the oversized and heavily insulated boots were called Mickey Mouse boots. My sergeant did not teach me much about my role in the field, because he done most of the work. If he called on me, I done whatever he said. If I was not working in our tent, I would be digging foxholes, pulling guard duty, or working at the dining facility.

Freezing and tired, it did not take long before I also lost my motivation and began to not care about my appearance. As I walked around, I wore my vest unsnapped and my Kevlar helmet was cocked on my head. My first sergeant told me to fix my gear because I looked like John Wayne. One night, I had to work the night shift and our pot belly stove stopped working. Our work tent was so cold that I thought I was going to die out there that night. A sergeant from California of all places saw how cold I was and told me to step outside the tent and start our HUMMV. He allowed me to sit inside the truck for a while to warm up. I spent twenty-one days in the mountains training in below freezing temperatures and I had never been so cold in my life; needless to say, I was glad when it ended.

Camp Hovey South Korea

CHAPTER 18

Private First Class Brown & Francisco

We drove back to our unit, unpacked, and cleaned our equipment and weapons. We then account for all sensitive items. This process took about three hours. Afterwards, the first sergeant allowed us to go to our rooms. The following day, I walked to the barbershop for a haircut. I was always wary of the barbers, not because they were Korean nationals, but because they were not good barbers. If I saw a soldier with a nice haircut, I would ask who had cut their hair? Sometimes, they had recently returned from the states, and the other times, it was someone in their unit who had cut their hair. If by chance it was a Korean national, I would ask for the barber's name, location, and which chair he or she used.

I met the soldier that lived next door to me. He was an infantry soldier that played country music every day. He played it so much that I memorized the lyrics. I also noticed the songs were sad, and although country music was not my favorite, I had listened to *Bonnie Raitt* before I joined the Army. I remembered liking her song *"I Can't Make You Love Me."*

As a private, I had to be physically fit, know my job, be on time, clean everything, and run errands. I also typed using a computer and a typewriter. The sergeants handwrote everything; because they had entered the Army during the late 1970s and 1980s, they knew little about computers. The day before payday, I drove to our finance office to pick up everyone's leave and earning statements (LES). This was what the military called a check stub. On payday, someone would hand them out. As a private (E-2), I earned seven hundred and fifty-four dollars a month. After work, most of the soldiers walked to the gym, but not me. I walked straight to my room, as I preferred to watch my thirteen-inch television, eat Korean food, and drink beer.

A few weeks later, I learned that my unit had a basketball team, so I joined. The coach held a practice session to figure out who would start. When he told me, "I would be coming off the bench," I did not like it. I knew there were others that were better than me, but I also knew he had favorites. On gameday, I did not play any during the first half. It wasn't until the middle of the second half when the coach called me to enter the game. I did not play defense, and on offense I ran around a *pick* and called for the ball. As soon as I touched the ball, I shot it. I was three feet behind the three-point line and the ball hit the top of the backboard. My coach called time-out, pulled me out of the game, and that was the last time I played for them.

I then joined our unit's flag football team; they were already 0-3 and the offense was horrible. We were 0-3, because our company commander was our quarterback, and he could not throw the football. Even though we complained, he would never relinquish the position. After losing the next game, I told them I could quarter-back; however, they did not believe me. At this point, we were 0-4, and the only way we could score was by handing the ball off. During the following game, someone said, "Let Hicks quarterback" and they did! I threw two touchdowns that day, and although we lost, it was the first time we scored through the air all season.

After the game, I met two other members on our team named PFC Francisco and PFC Brown. Francisco was a cool brother from Decatur, Georgia. He was an infantryman and seemed like a good soldier. He was physically fit, and he did not drink or smoke. I began using ketchup on my scrambled eggs because of him. Brown was from Brooklyn, New York, and his career field was communications. He was married with a child, older than us, and caught one of the touchdowns I threw. Brown and I began to drink Blue Bulls at our Quonset huts. I also drunk Soju, the most popular liquor in South Korea. It was a clear liquor and contained twenty percent alcohol. I paid five dollars for a two-liter bottle, that I mixed with orange or cranberry juice. It tasted good!

One night, Brown and I walked outside the back gates of Camp Hovey to a local Korean bar just to see what it was like. It was just like the small bars in the states, so we sat down, watched television, and drank beer. On our way back, we walked through an alley filled with closed businesses, and Brown dared me to throw a brick through a window. When I did, the window shattered, and a Korean man ran from inside the store and began cursing at us. We quickly ran off and made it back to our rooms. A few moments later, someone knocked on my door and told me to report to our company headquarters. When I walked through the door, my first sergeant told me that a business owner filed a report about a broken window, and when the gate guard checked the logbook, it showed me and Brown signing in after the incident occurred. I denied having anything to do with it and he eventually let me go back to my room. The following day, a sergeant approached me and said that he was in a meeting with our first sergeant, and the first sergeant told them that I was trouble and that I needed to be watched. I thanked him, and from that point forward, anytime I saw my first sergeant, he looked at me with a frown.

Several weeks later, Brown and I caught the local shuttle bus or the ten-minute ride from Camp Hovey to Camp Casey's main gate. When we arrived, we walked out the gate onto the main road. We then crossed the road and walked over a set of train tracks, where we saw a small crowd of soldiers huddled together. We walked over and noticed the soldiers lining up to punch something like a heavy bag. It looked like the scene from the movie Rocky IV, where the Russian punched a heavy bag and a machine calculated how hard he punched it. We watched as the soldiers punched the bag hard and they all received good scores. But when Brown stepped up, he shattered everyone's score with one punch. When we walked off, Brown said that he was a boxer. I believed him.

On another occasion, a few other soldiers, Brown, and I were drinking beer outside of our huts, and as I was doing pushups on the sidewalk, I could see Brown conversating with another soldier. Their conversation seemed serious, but I did not care, so jokingly I said to Brown, "Man shut the fu$$ up, you don't know what you're talking about!" As I continued to joke, he ignored me, but later that night, I heard a knock on my door. When I opened the door it was Brown. He said, "If you ever speak to me like that again, I will fu$$ you up." I told him that I was just joking but he was not. He then stormed out of my Quonset hut, and we stopped speaking; however, two months later, Francisco brought us back together and we all began to hang out again.

CHAPTER 19

Uniform Code of Military Justice

After five months of this tour, I bought a round trip ticket for eight hundred and fifty-three dollars and flew back home for thirty days. I saw my brother, Quanta, Ms. Martinez, Detective Black, Jamal, and hung out with friends from JDUB. When my leave was over, I returned to my unit and to a two-week field exercise which was not that bad. Days after returning from the field, I rode the bus for two hours to Yongsan/Seoul South Korea. The interstates were like the ones in the United States and the South Koreans drove fast. As we drove closer to the city, the traffic became very congested. Police officers stood in the middle of the road to monitor and control traffic.

The moped riders showed no fear. They rode in and out of traffic between the largest vehicles. I also noticed that in the congested areas, the larger vehicles bullied everyone on the road. The larger trucks and buses would cut in front of the smaller cars forcing them to stop. The South Koreans only drove a version of the Hyundai, and if I saw another type of vehicle (e.g., Lexus), it belonged to an

American. We arrived on-post and parked at the bus station. I then walked outside the main gates and down the street to shop. After I finished shopping, I walked back to the post for a haircut, and this time the barber had done a good job. Part of the experience included a shoulder massage, and the barber cracked our necks. While I was at Camp Hovey, we either ate at the dining facility, ordered pizza, or ordered Korean food, but on Yongsan's main post, they had an Anthony's Pizza, Burger King, a Chinese restaurant, Robinhood and a few other restaurants. Korean nationals worked there, and the restaurants were exceptionally clean. I sat down, ate, and watched service members and some families from all branches come and go. Afterwards, I walked back to the bus terminal. As soon as I opened the terminal' front door, straight ahead was a popcorn and cookie stand. So, I bought six oatmeal raisin cookies and boarded the bus for Camp Hovey.

At work, my load was light, and I always looked forward to Friday evenings; because, even if I did not have any money, I could always find a drink. One Friday night, Brown and I convinced two soldiers to go outside Camp Casey's main gate with us. We walked down the alley going in and out of every club there. The clubs were dark inside and lit with disco balls. They played a variety of music and had different flavors of Soju. As we walked through the crowded alley, a guy bumped into someone I was with, and it led to an argument. It was four of them against four of us, and when someone swung a punch, it was on. We punched them and they punched us back. I tripped a guy to the ground and punched him a couple of times. Then someone pulled me off him and said, "Hicks we got to go." When I stood up and looked around, I saw one of the guys that I was with stand over a guy and stump on his face. We tried to flee but there was nowhere to hide. The military police patrolled the outside gates and arrived quickly. They walked us all to the on-post police station for questioning. The military police then called our company headquarters and the sergeant on duty picked us up. The next morning, I had to see my first sergeant. I explained what happened and admitted to fighting. He said the soldier that was stumped on needed stitches, and I told him that "I was not the one who had done that." I also did not tell him who had done it, but none of that mattered; because this was an excellent opportunity for my first sergeant to discipline me.

In the military, The Uniform Code of Military Justice (UCMJ) governed us. It was our federal law book, and it gave commanders the authority to discipline servicemembers. I received what was known as a Summarized Article 15. The punishment included extra duty for fourteen days, and a written reprimand. Since I was a private, they did not take any money from me. Extra duty began after work at 1700 hours and lasted until midnight. For my extra duty, I had to pick weeds out of sidewalks, cut the grass, build pullup bars, clean offices, and toilets, empty the trash, sweep, mop and repeatedly strip and wax the floors.

A few weeks later, there was a promotion ceremony, and as I watched my peers advance, I stood there feeling like a failure. For me to earn a promotion, I had to change, and change I did. The first week I arrived at my unit, my supervisor enrolled me into the Army Correspondence Course Program. The program used official Army training doctrine and turned them into testable courses (e.g., first aid, Army promotions, map reading, marching, UCMJ, land navigation). There were hundreds of different courses to take, and I had immediately begun to enroll in them over the computer. However, when the yellow booklets arrived through the mail, I threw them inside my wall locker. I had no excuse not to begin to work on them. There were several young sergeants that had the correct answers, and they were more than willing to share them. Once I completed a booklet, I mailed the answer key back for grading, and within a few weeks, I would receive a document in the mail stating that I had passed. I then began to build my own answer keys to help others.

In addition to this change, I got a new first sergeant which allowed me a fresh start, and it helped. I began driving for our battalion commander who was a lieutenant colonel (LTC). I drove a 1993 Hyundai Sonata and I enjoyed it; because it gave me a chance to see more of the country and this was great. Being a driver also helped to take my mind off being homesick. While the LTC was attending his meetings, I stayed in the car, because I did not feel comfortable around senior leadership.

On the weekends, my captain also needed a driver, and since Private Sanchez and I were the only two privates in the office, this meant that we were his designated weekend drivers. Private Sanchez knew how to drive a stick shift, but I did not. Our captain was fair, and he did not want Sanchez to have to drive him every time he had to go somewhere. So, one Friday evening, the captain told me to meet him at the office on Saturday morning by 0800 hours. I said yes sir, and at 0745 hours that Saturday morning, I walked into the office and retrieved the keys and vehicle paperwork. The captain gave me a quick class on how to use the gears and clutch. I started the pickup truck and became comfortable with the gears. I struggled pulling off, but I did not have a problem shifting gears. We made it to the Camp Casey Post Exchange safely, and I was relieved.

The captain shopped and I stayed in the truck. When it was time to leave, I had to drive up a hill, balance the accelerator and clutch, and wait until I had a chance to pull onto the main highway. When I had a chance to do so, I put the truck in first gear, gently lifted my foot off the clutch and mashed on the accelerator. The engine roared and we rolled backwards twenty yards. Fortunately, there was no one behind us. I slowly drove back to the top of the hill, correctly balanced the clutch and accelerator, and pulled off. We safely made it back to our unit. A couple of days later, I learned I was on assignment to Fort Campbell, Kentucky. When I asked my sergeants about Fort Campbell, they never said anything positive about the place. On January 1, 1995, I was eligible for promotion and earned the rank of specialist (E-4). I was happy, and three days later, I flew back to the states.

CHAPTER 20

Fort Campbell, Kentucky

While I was in South Korea, I asked Quanta to marry me, and she said yes. I was thrilled. Now that I had returned, it was time to talk to Ms. Janet about our pending marriage. She recommended that we wait, but not because she was against it, but because Quanta and I were so young. I was twenty-one, and she was nineteen. However, we continued to press the issue until she gave us the OKAY, and on January 20, 1995, we were married in Portsmouth at the Justice of Peace. Our family members and friends showed up, and we appreciated it. I realized that I was still new to the Army, and I knew even less about marriage, but I knew that I wanted to marry Quanta. I often thought about her asking me, "If I had ever considered the military as an option?" It was her suggestion that had persuaded me to join the military which had put me in a better situation. Although I started off screwing up when I first joined the Army, I was now doing well. I had a career, a steady paycheck, a roof over my head, and I wanted Quanta to enjoy this journey right along with me.

Jan 20, 1995 - Married

Shortly after the wedding, I reported to Fort Campbell, and since I did not know what to expect, I suggested Quanta remain home. I bought a bus ticket and rode a Greyhound bus from Portsmouth to Fort Campbell, Kentucky which was in Clarksville, Tennessee. It was a long ride. I believe I rode a taxi from the bus station to Fort Campbell's Reception Station. When I arrived, I met a soldier named PFC Warren who was from Hampton, Virginia. When I told him I was from Portsmouth, it was on. A few days later we had a four-day weekend, and since we were in-processing, we were supposed to remain local. We did not. In fact, we rented a car off post, disabled the odometer, and drove to Virginia. PFC Johnson also rode with us. We had also met him at the reception station, and he was from North Carolina. I wanted to be the first to drive, because I did not trust anyone's driving. We drove off around 1600 hours. That night it was very foggy. As I drove, I looked behind me and there were no vehicles insight, and since this was the case, I used the entire road and drove between the lines. Suddenly, I saw blue lights flashing and I woke the guys up. I tucked the half-filled beer can behind my seat and pulled over. As I grabbed the steering wheel with both hands, I held my credentials as well. The police officer asked for my license and registration. I handed it to him along with my military identification. He asked why I was driving between the lanes, and I explained that I could not see, and since there wasn't anyone behind me, I used the entire road. The police officer recommended that I not do that, and he did not give me a ticket.

I continued driving but I had begun to feel tired, so I pulled over and PFC Johnson began to drive. As I sat in the back seat, I did not go to sleep. Instead, I watched his driving and noticed his eyes closing. I asked him if he was all right, and he said yes, but he was not, so I asked him to pull over. PFC Warren wanted to drive but I told him that I was fine. I dropped Johnson off in North Carolina so he could get his car. I continued to Portsmouth. It was a fifteen hour drive. I spent the next two days at home, and when it was time to return to Kentucky, I drove my Hyundai back to Fort Campbell and Warren drove the rental car.

The reception station sent me to HHC, 187th Infantry Regiment, where my first sergeant allowed me to sign for a room in our barracks since there were rooms available. That night, I learned about a club on-post called Champions. I drove there, and it was nice. I ended up staying there until 0145 hours, although the club closed at 0200 hours. I drove back to my barracks and fell asleep. Hours later, I heard someone knocking on my door. When I woke up, I realized that I had missed my very first formation with my new unit. Smelling of alcohol, I staggered to the door, opened it and the sergeant standing there introduced himself as my supervisor. I apologized for missing the formation and he forgave me.

My unit gave me ten days off to find an apartment. Once I found an apartment, I rode a Greyhound bus back to Portsmouth and rented the largest U-Haul truck available. Quanta's uncle had given us his old but hardly used furniture. It was nice and we appreciated it. I had never driven a truck that size before, but I was not too concerned. I was a good driver, I knew how to read a map, and I had Quanta with me. Along the way, we stopped for gas at a small-town gas station somewhere in Kentucky. Quanta had stayed in the truck, and I entered the store and walked the aisles looking for junk food. I was wearing a large Arizona Cardinals pullover that I bought from South Korea. There was a zipper pouch in front large enough to carry a textbook. When I walked to the counter to pay, the White man told me to empty my pockets, because the front of my jacket bulged, and he thought I had stolen something. As white people watched, I knew I had stopped in the wrong small town. I unzipped the pouch and removed everything. I carried my Walkman, headphones, wallet, paperwork, truck keys, and other things. I had not stolen anything. I paid for our gas and walked out of the store. I told Quanta what happened, and I drove off. We safely arrived at our apartment and began to unpack.

CHAPTER 21

Air Assault School

I reported back to my unit and began working. I met the soldiers I worked with, and they were OKAY. In our building, we had pictures of past commanders hanging on the walls. We also had pictures and plaques of past wars we were a part of. They dated back to World War II (1939-1945). I began to take notice of soldiers in our unit. They walked and talked with pride and were noticeably confident. If someone asked them a question, they responded with Rakkasan. That was our unit's nickname.

Fort Campbell was the home of the 101st Airborne Division. It was also the home of The Air Assault School. In my unit, it was an absolute must that every soldier completed Air Assault School. If not, a soldier was considered a dud and receiving a promotion was not an option. I never told anyone that I was afraid of heights; because I knew speaking about it would not keep me from going. I reported to the Air Assault School at 0430 hours and there were already more than fifty soldiers waiting. We formed up and done lower body exercises on gravel. Then we done pull-ups and completed a two-mile run wearing our battle dress uniform (BDU) pants and running shoes. Immediately afterwards, I neatly laid out over thirty items for inspection in front of the school. If I would have forgotten one item, I would have been dropped from the course. With half of them being challenging, we then walked to complete a challenging obstacle course.

We lined up facing away and behind an obstacle and were given two attempts to complete each obstacle. I found the thirty-five feet wooden ladder separated by ten wooden beams incredibly challenging. I had to climb to the top and over it, and the higher I climbed, the distance between each beam increased. When I reached the top, I was shaking like a leaf, near muscle failure and physically exhausted. There was an instructor sitting between the wooden beams near the top. He looked at me and knew that I was nervous. He said something to motivate me, and I continued down. If I would have fallen off the ladder, I would have hit the ground not a net. After this event, we ate MREs, and waited for the results from the day. There were over a dozen soldiers who were asked not to return. I was not one of them. So, I drove home and took a shower. This was the beginning of day zero.

Upon returning, the instructors had us sit in a classroom. Before we began training, the instructors asked, "Who was with the 187th Infantry?" I raised my hand and so did a few others. We were told not to say Rakkasan while in school. It had been banned from being said on school grounds, because we said the word so much. Instead, we all yelled Air Assault. For the first two days, I learned how to prepare and transport cargo (e.g., supplies, vehicles) from one point to another. We also used old Army helicopters to learn how to rappel. In the days to come, we would be expected to rappel from a fifty feet tower with and without *gear*.

On that day and in a single file line, each soldier lined up at the base of the tower. Once we climbed to the top we had to stand with our backs looking away from soldiers that were rappelling. As I looked around, I became lightheaded and kneeled. I stood back up and nervously waited until it was my turn to practice. The instructor told me to face him and kneel. He then connected the metal clamp I wore to his and I stood up. I carefully backed closer to the edge of the wall. With the heels of my feet hanging off the edge, I bent my knees and *pushed* away from the wall while loosening the rope behind my back, and I repeated this until I reached the bottom. Next, we put on our gloves and practiced free falling from the top of the tower. We had to jump off the tower onto a rope and ride it down. The next day, the instructors graded us on the proper technique to rappel, and unfortunately for me, I did not do it correctly and failed. Therefore, the school sent me back to my unit and I was considered a dud.

A month later, my unit sent me back and I was able to correctly rappel. So, I remained in the course and continued. The instructors had us load up in a UH-60 Blackhawk Helicopter. We flew all over the post with the doors open while the pilot made fast hard turns. I closed my eyes, held my weapon, and remained stiff as a board during the duration of the flight. The following day, it was turn to rappel from the side of the Blackhawk. I boarded the helicopter, sat down, and fastened my seat belt. The helicopter lifted one hundred feet in the air and hovered in place. As I sat, I watched two soldiers' rappel, and they made it look easy. The instructor told me that I was next, so I unfastened my seat belt, stood up, stepped forward and kneeled. Once the sergeant connected my metal clamp to his, I stood up, turned around, inched closer to the edge, placed the toe of my boots on the base of the helicopter and loosened the rope behind my back. The winds from the helicopter were strong, which made my vest, rucksack, and weapon heavier. I looked over my shoulder and said, "Oh sh$$!" It was a long way down. When the instructor looked at me and said, "GO!," I did not move. He then looked at me as if he was mad, and this time when he said go, I pushed off and slowly lowered myself to the ground. The next day, I completed a twelve-mile road march in full gear with my weapon and graduated earning my Air Assault wings.

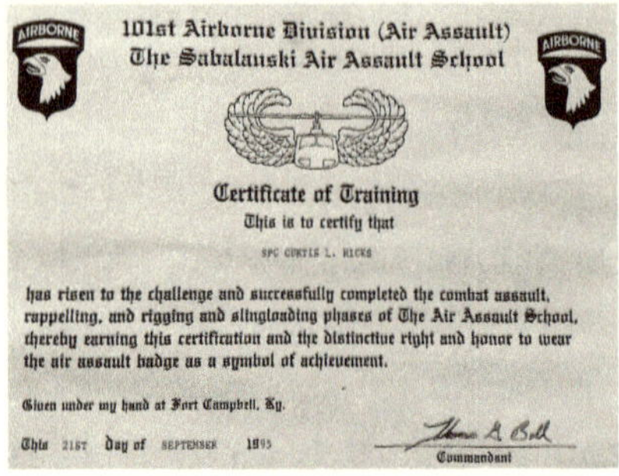

Air Assault Certificate

CHAPTER 22

Back Forty

Quanta began working on post at Kentucky Fried Chicken (KFC), and since she worked early in the morning, I dropped her off on my way to physical training. Afterwards, I drove back for free breakfast. Quanta had a coworker named Tammy who was cool, and later I met her husband, PFC Miles. I learned that they were from Detroit, and that we all lived in the same neighborhood; therefore, we became good friends. There was not much to do in Clarksville, Tennessee and Quanta and I spent most of our time working. We called home often, but in 1995, there was no such thing as a phone plan, and since the phone company charged long distance calls by the minute it was costly.

Months later, I learned that Cameron had joined the Army and was also stationed at Fort Campbell. We had grown up in JDUB together, so once we connected it was on. On Saturdays, he would visit Quanta and I at our apartment. Him and I ate well, drank beer, and hung out. I also introduced him to PFCs Warren, Gilbert, Miles, Johnson and SPC Clock and Reed. We all began to hang out and have fun. On Sundays, we watched sports and done more drinking.

One day while I was at work, I had to drive over to our finance office to drop off some paperwork, but before I walked into the building, I saw a soldier that I was with in basic training. He had stayed far away from me during training: however, on this day he looked at me and said, "I cannot believe you're still in the Army." I spoke, gave a slight grin, and kept walking. He was right, I had been a pain in the a$$ in basic training.

A few months later, my battalion began to prepare for a thirty-day field exercise. Two days prior to the exercise we packed, and the next morning we formed a convoy, and slowly drove forty-five minutes to the site. We referred to this exceptionally large training site as the Back Forty. When we arrived, we had to secure the area and set up communications, pull guard duty, set up medium size work and sleep tents, dig fox holes, cut down tall grass, put up concertina wire, fire up the generators, and schedule twelve hours work shifts. Just like South Korea!

To a degree, we simulated training, and my main responsibility was to keep our unit's strength at ninety percent or higher. There were at least four units in our battalion and each unit began at one hundred percent strengthen. If a soldier were injured, I would send them a soldier with the same military occupational specialty (MOS) and skill set. For example, if a unit lost a 71L10, the 71L was the MOS and the 10 was the skill set.

I also done night Air Assault missions. When called upon, I would grab my gear and ride in a HUMMV to a remote area where there would be an old Army pickup truck in the field. My battle buddy and I would prepare the truck to be carried off. Afterwards, we told war stories, played cards, ate MREs, and waited. I also prayed. Once we received word that we were going live, we put on our gear, and I positioned myself ten yards slightly to the right of the pickup truck. When we heard the CH-47 Army Chinook (This was a heavy lift helicopter that carried personnel and equipment.) heading our way, dressed in gloves, goggles, ear plugs, Kevlar, and vest, we waited until the chinook hoovered over the truck. From an angle, my battle buddy and I mounted the truck with the chinook now hovering over our heads. Inside the bed of the truck was a heavy metal hook and a long pole. I picked up the pole known as a static probe, and he picked up the metal hook. Then I placed the static probe against another piece of metal underneath the chinook. My battle buddy then connected his hook to the bottom of the chinook. I could not remove the static probe until he connected the hook. If I did, once he attached the hook, the electrical shock would have killed him. Now that the hook was connected, I removed the static probe and placed it back into the truck. We dismounted and the chinook flew off. Although nervous, I had learned to trust my training and my battle buddies. We worked as a team and depended on each other to succeed. I rode back to our field site feeling accomplished.

Days later, the field exercise ended and although it was the best news I had heard in weeks, it was raining. Once we packed everything up and accounted for all our sensitive items, we drove back to our unit. We unpacked and spent hours cleaning our equipment and weapons. To sham a little, I volunteered to drive to the wash rack to wash our HUMMV and trailer. Afterwards, I felt exhausted and frustrated, and once I turned onto the main road, I aggressively mashed down on the accelerator. When I removed my foot, the truck continued to accelerate. I applied the brakes, and it would not slow down. I said, "Oh sh$$!" Luckily as I looked ahead there were no vehicles in front of me; however, there were soldiers walking around. To the right was a large parade field, so I pulled over, continued to mash on the brakes, pulled up on the emergency brake, and the truck finally began to slow down and eventually stopped. When I put the HUMMV in park, the engine roared as if the HUMMV was still in motion. I turned the truck off, and the engine stopped roaring. A minute later, I started the HUMMV, and it sounded normal, so I *slowly* drove back to my unit.

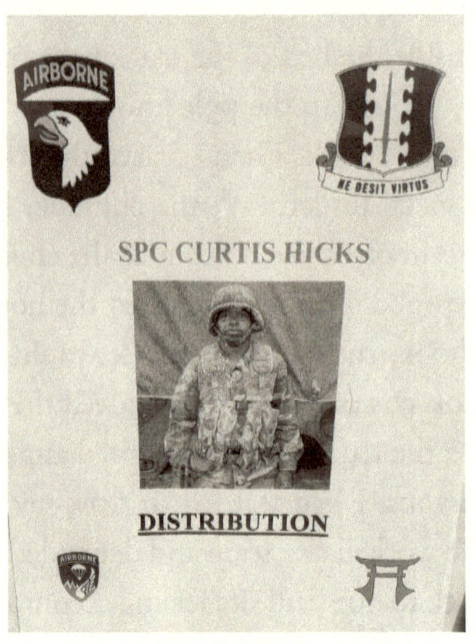

Specialist Hicks

CHAPTER 23

That Was Funny

Quanta landed another job at the dining facility on post, and it was going well. However, on one Friday evening, while I was at Specialist Warren's house drinking beer, I called Jason and he spoke about an incident that was overly concerning to me. That night, Warren and I drove to Portsmouth. I picked up my brother, and he returned to live with us at Fort Campbell. Jason started working and later met my battle buddies. I had talked about our upbringing so much that the soldiers started calling me *JDUB*.

On the job, things were still the same. I done physical training and worked long hours. Every month my unit required me to wear my Army dress uniform. On this day, my supervisor told me to run an errand. I said, "Rakkasan," and walked to our company head-quarters. When I entered the building, I saw my first sergeant stand-ing in the hallway. As I stood at parade rest, he asked me, "If anyone had inspected my uniform?" I said, "No first sergeant." He replied with, "I can tell because you look like a piece of sh$$. Now get the fu$$ out my building." He then called my supervisor and cursed him out. I did not take pride in wearing my uniform and it showed. I walked back to our office and sat down with Sergeant Thomas who was our paralegal and reenlistment sergeant. He worked in our office twice a week and was sharp. He helped me with my uniform, and I appreciated it. We began to talk a little more and eventually became good friends. After work, he played basketball and asked if I wanted to go, and I did. I began to care more about my appearance. I dry cleaned my uniforms, and spit shined my boots. When I wore my dress uniform, I cleaned my brass belt buckle very well. My job performance also improved, especially in the field.

We trained in the field every ninety days, and each time the training exercises lasted for thirty days. With so much field training, I became a subject matter expert in the woods. Sergeants began to call on me to take charge and I did. While my role was important, the infantry soldiers had incredibly challenging missions. On one training exercise, there was a squad on a mission, and they were carrying live rounds and grenades. Once they counted their sensitive items, they noticed a grenade was missing. The platoon leader informed his chain of command, and someone called our explosive ordnance division (EOD). At this point, EOD had to find the grenade. While the squad was waiting for EOD to arrive, they began looking for the grenade. As they done this, a soldier stepped on the grenade. It detonated, and regrettably one soldier died.

Fort Campbell Back 40 Training Site /
Specialist Hicks

CHAPTER 24

Reenlistment

Army life at Fort Campbell was challenging, but to balance things out, my friends and I drove to Nashville, Tennessee to see the **W**itty **U**npredictable **T**alent **A**nd **N**atural **G**ame Clan concert (Wu Tang Clan). They were my favorite hip hop group, and everyone knew it. After the concert, security allowed us to exit out the back door. I walked out and saw the minivan the Wu was driving. As I looked around, Ghostface Killa who was a member of the group walked out the back door. I walked up to him and asked him for his autograph, and he said yes. He had a pen, so I handed him a piece of paper. He then said, "Yeah son, let me sign this with my murder weapon." I smiled, thanked him, and told him I was from Portsmouth, Virginia, because they had a Wu Wear store there. I shook his hand and walked off happy. My friends and I spent the rest of the night drinking, joking, and making a scene wherever we went. That was a fun night.

The following week, I spoke with Sergeant Thomas about reenlisting. My contract was expiring, and I knew I was staying in the Army, because I had no other plans. Plus, the sooner I reenlisted, the sooner I could leave Fort Campbell. I told Sergeant Thomas I wanted to be stationed in Virginia. He said, "OKAY," and a few weeks later, he said that "Fort Lee, Virginia was available." I accepted the assignment and reenlisted for another four years.

While Quanta and I were excited, leaving my unit was not that easy. My unit was planning to fly to Fort Irwin, California for a thirty-day training exercise. If they wanted to, my unit could delay my assignment until our mission was completed; however, on one Friday evening, my captain called me into his office. I stood outside of his door at the position of attention, until he told me to enter. He wanted me to go with our unit to Fort Irwin, because I was their most experienced soldier. Instead of telling me I could not leave for Fort Lee, he allowed me to make the decision. He told me to speak with my wife about it and let him know on Monday. I said, "Rakkasan, sir.," and drove home. On Monday morning, I told the captain that we wanted to leave for Virginia. He was fine with it, and we never spoke about it again.

One morning after physical training, the captain called me into his office again. Visibly shaken, he handed me a piece of paper and asked if I knew anything about it. The note written in crayon read:

"I cannot believe you allowed Specialist Hicks to make this decision. Since when do we let soldiers make these types of decisions? All Specialist Hicks wants to do is stay in the rear and drink beer."

The captain had found the note underneath his door. I said sir, I did not write this, but I knew who did. It was my sergeant first class. I knew his handwriting. Later that morning, Sergeant Thomas asked me, "If I wanted the incident investigated?" and I said, "No." But I did ask him to help me leave at my scheduled time and he did. My unit released me in April of 1997. Quanta and I drove back to Virginia while Jason remained in Tennessee where he lived with SPC Warren and continued to work at Opryland in Nashville.

My First Reenlistment

CHAPTER 25

Fort Lee Main Post Office

In May of 1997, Quanta and I drove from Portsmouth to Fort Lee, Virginia. The drive took an hour and twenty minutes. When we arrived, we discovered that it was a small training post. The reception station assigned me to a headquarters detachment, and I worked at the main post office. The post did not have any infantry units and I loved that. The sergeants seemed calmer and did not curse every time they spoke. My primary job was to deliver unofficial mail on post, and I also inspected unit mail rooms for compliance. At work I collaborated with civilians and soldiers. One of the soldiers was a guy named Specialist George. When we saw each other, we smiled. We had completed basic training together and it was good to see him. I also met a cool soldier named Specialist Tate. He was married and from Georgia. I would learn that we all enjoyed drinking, playing video games, and gambling because that's exactly what we done.

A couple of months later, I was eligible for promotion; however, there was something holding me back...my gut. I was overweight. One day, my first sergeant called me into his office and spoke to me about my weight. He said, the longer I stayed out of tolerance, the longer I was cutting my money short. I understood and said,

"Hooah, (which was Army slang) First Sergeant." I drove to our post exchange (GNC) and bought their most popular weight loss supplement. I began to watch what I ate and exercised after work. In two months, I lost thirty-five pounds. I passed my physical fitness test, and my unit sent me to school.

I drove to Fort Knox, Kentucky to attend the Primary Leadership Development Course (PLDC). The course was a month long, and it taught the fundamentals of leadership, training, and war fighting. There was a mixture of classroom and outdoor instructions. We learned how to do things such as lead a physical training session and march a squad from one location to another. PLDC was not challenging, however, at the end of the course, there was a three-day field exercise. As we tactically road marched to the site, there were large deer running around. We arrived and spent the day training. After each training session, the instructors graded us. On day two, we had to complete a land navigation course. This discipline required us to follow a route on foot through unfamiliar terrain while using a map of the land, a compass, and other navigational tools. Since we were in training, as a precautionary measure we carried whistles. As I stood in the middle of condensed woods, I circled the four locations on my map I had to find and walked off. I found my first location with ease. The next one was farther away and through rougher terrain. As I pushed tree branches out of my face, I walked into a spider web and lost my composure. I closed my eyes and wiped across my face. Then I opened my eyes and made sure there were no spiders on me. Once I regained my composure, I realized I had forgotten my pace count. A pace count was how we measured distance from one known point to another. Additionally, when I looked around, all I saw were tall trees. Every direction looked the same.

As I continued to walk, I became frustrated and fatigued. I then realized that I had approached an extremely steep cliff. I looked over the cliff and became lightheaded. I turned around, walked in the opposite direction, and yelled, "HELP!" I blew my whistle, but no one responded. I walked another five minutes before I knew where I was. I failed land navigation. However, the next day, I received a second try, and I found all my points. I graduated from PLDC and returned to Fort Lee.

PLDC Graduation - Specialist Hicks

A month later, I earned the rank of sergeant. I was happy and thanked my supervisor Sergeant Jensen because she always encouraged me to do well. With the promotion my responsibility increased a little, and my peers were supportive. They were my friends and I appreciated that.

CHAPTER 26

My Homeboy

On the weekends, I drove to Portsmouth and connected with my homeboy Midnight. We bought beer, ate fried crabs, and watched old school Kung Fu movies. I loved it. One day, we spoke, and he told me that his job was planning to work near Fort Lee. Since the job would take them months to complete, he would stay in a hotel. I said, "That was great, and I looked forward to that time." Midnight arrived and worked Monday through Friday, and on Friday evenings, I picked him up. We bought a twelve pack of beer and a bottle of liquor, and I drove to my house. Quanta knew him from school and was happy to see him. Even though we had fun, Midnight missed his family and I completely understood. Quanta and I lived in a two-bedroom house on post, so I spoke with Quanta about his family living with us until he completed his job, and she was fine with it. I asked Midnight, and he loved the idea. Several weeks later, he and his family moved in. Now instead of driving home every weekend, Midnight and I stayed at Fort Lee. Specialist Tate lived two blocks away from me, so we all brought our wives together and we had a great time.

One weekend, Midnight had to work. I convinced Tate to ride to Portsmouth with me. Tate met Jamal and Cameron and we all spent the day drinking and joking. That night, I was driving a little too fast, back to Fort Lee, and I passed a state trooper driving in the opposite direction. The police officer cut on his lights, made a U turn, and pursued me. I was like oh sh$$. I had never had a problem with hiding a beer can, but it was hard to hide the open twelve-pack of beer between Tate's legs. The officer asked for my license and registration. He saw the beer and asked questions. I told the police officer it was me drinking and not Tate. The officer allowed Tate to drive home, and he drove me to jail. Hours later, Quanta bailed me out. Although Quanta was mad and I felt bad, that was the least of my concerns. Once my unit found out, I would be dishonorably discharged, but I had an idea.

CHAPTER 27

Human Resource Professionals

In my unit, we were all human resource soldiers. These professionals served in positions I had never heard of before and most had never been in an infantry unit. They taught me to not wait for the Army to tell me where I was going and that the Department of the Army was in northern Virginia. This was where my career counselor worked. I also knew that if we wanted to, we could drive there, sit down with a counselor, and ask for our next duty station. My peers also told me that there were a handful of civilians there locally with the same authority. So, on Monday morning, I drove to the building where the civilians worked, sat down with a lady, and asked if I could be placed on assignment? After she checked, she said that "I had not been there long enough to move." As I looked hopeless, she continued to check. Then she said, "If I agreed to complete postal school at Fort Jackson, I could leave for South Korea soon after." Postal school was just two months away, so I agreed.

The next day, I contacted the court and spoke to someone about my school obligation. When the clerk asked me when I would finish school, the date I gave her had me already in South Korea. That would be my new court date.

I drove to Fort Jackson to complete postal school. It was a five-week course that taught me how to work as a window clerk. I learned how to sell money orders, safeguard registered mail, find suspicious packages, and other things. It was not difficult, but I had to take it seriously, because if I lost a book of stamps, I had to pay for it, and if my cash account was inaccurate, I had to pay the difference out of my pocket. On August 12, 1998, I graduated from postal school. I returned to my unit and continued to work. I do not know why but before my court date the civilian authorities never contacted anyone at Fort Lee, and I was thankful. In November of 1998, I flew back to South Korea, and to save money, Quanta stayed with her mom until I returned.

US Army Postal School

CHAPTER 28

Incheon South Korea (Camp Market)

When I arrived in South Korea, the reception station sent me to Delta Company, 516th Adjutant General Battalion where my unit worked at the main post office. Since I knew my way around, I walked to the post office. I introduced myself and met my supervisor. She told me that I would be working at Kimpo International Airport. She drove me there and I met a couple of my soldiers. I also collaborated with civilians and Air Force personnel. There was a section of the airport appointed for processing mail. When the planes arrived, shortly after, large metal containers filled with mail would be transported to our area. We unloaded the mail and placed it on conveyor belts. There were three or more eighteen-wheeler trucks parked outside. Soldiers filled the trucks with mail and rode with Korean nationals to deliver it. The trucks returned and the process started over. It was nice to meet them all.

I lived thirty minutes from the airport at a place called Camp Market. I signed for a barrack's room and met the rest of my soldiers. There were no more than fifty soldiers and civilians living out there.

We had the entire camp to ourselves. We worked six days a week and the first shift began at 0500 hours. We drove either a minivan or a five-speed truck to work. I enjoyed my soldiers and the job. For those soldiers that had not done so, I made them enroll in the Army Correspondence Courses Program.

A couple of weeks later, Quanta mailed me paperwork saying that they had charged me with driving under the influence (DUI), and that I had lost my license for a year. After a year, I could have my license reinstated, but I would have to pay a large fine and keep the proper insurance. A charge like this normally would quickly catch up with a soldier, but I never heard from anyone, and I was thankful yet again.

Private First Class Garcia, Fitzgerald, and Hernandez were three of my favorite soldiers. We all worked well together. PFC Hernandez was from DC and had a connection to Portsmouth. He did not drink or smoke and was a fan of the singer Prince. We ate out at restaurants, played basketball, watched Kung Fu, and clubbed. I also reconnected with Sergeant Gilbert from Fort Campbell. He was also in South Korea but hours away. One weekend, he visited Camp Market, met my soldiers, and we all rode the train to Yongsan. We partied half the night and had fun.

Every Thursday, we had mandatory sergeant's time training, and since our training was tailored to our current mission, we trained more on topics related to the post office. After riding in the truck with my soldiers, I knew they were not good drivers. To break up the monotony this Thursday, we practiced how to drive the five-speed truck on Camp Market. Safety was always my number one concern. I completed a risk assessment and had my supervisor approve it. That day my soldiers and I met at the truck, but before driving, they each inspected the vehicle for damage. Underneath the driver's side sun visor, we kept a green binder with paperwork. Whatever damage was found, we wrote it on this paperwork. The most experienced soldiers drove first. It was a five-minute drive around the camp, and it ended at a stop sign. We would then switch drivers and he/she did the same. I had never seen this one soldier drive before, so I asked him, "If he knew how to drive?" and he said, "Yes sergeant." Like every soldier, he inspected the outside of the truck, and found no damage. He entered the vehicle, fastened his seat belt, and started the truck. I told Private Goldberg we were going to make a right and he said, "Yes, Sergeant." He put the gear in first, turned the steering wheel to the right and pulled off fast. He continued to turn the steering wheel to the right and never straightened it. He drove onto the sidewalk and slammed into a large tree. In shock, he kept his foot on the accelerator and the engine roared. I tried to calm him, but it did not work. There was another soldier sitting in the back seat, who tried to move the gear from first to neutral, but when he did, he was electrically shocked. Private Goldberg eventually calmed down and removed his foot off the accelerator. We all received minor cuts and bruises, and I reported the accident to my supervisor. Afterwards, I spoke with my soldier, and he said he could not drive. There was a girl in our unit that he liked, and since she was there at sergeant's time training, he did not want her to know that he could not drive. We were extremely fortunate, because there was a restaurant there and people normally stood on that same sidewalk daily.

I was in my room one weekend, and when I opened my door, I noticed an unfamiliar sergeant first class drinking a beer. He looked like a weightlifter and was there visiting someone. Later that day, he overheard us talking trash about playing basketball. As usual, it led to us going to the gym. The sergeant first class wanted to play and walked over with us. We began with a game of twenty-one and then three on three. The sergeant first class and I were on separate teams and guarded each other. I made a layup and talked trash. I hit two jump shots and talked even more. The last shot was a game winning long jumper in his face. In celebration, I jumped in the air, mean mugged him, and told him he sucked. He did not like that and was ready to fight. I was not backing down, and when I stepped towards him, PFC Hernandez stepped between us. I was glad because a few weeks prior, I asked my unit if I could bring Quanta over and they approved her travel. This was not typical. I did not want to screw up.

Quanta received her passport and flew over. I met her at the airport, and we caught a taxi to the Yongsan main post where I showed her around. Then we caught the train to Camp Market and walked to our barracks building. We did not live in the same barracks as my soldiers, because I had moved into another barracks made for senior personnel. Our new room had a full bathroom, a stove, and an oven.

The next day, we wanted to go shopping. It was a forty-five-minute train ride from Camp Market to Yongsan, so we walked on the already full train, and were the only Americans onboard. Quanta wore nice-looking braids and drew a lot of attention. The locals loved her hair and stared in amazement. As we continued, Quanta said she was hot, and it was hard to breathe. A few moments later, Quanta said that she felt like she was going to pass out. I held her upright, and when the train stopped, she struggled to walk off. The fresh air and cold water helped. Afterwards, we rode a taxi to Yongsan main post, ate Korean food, and properly hydrated. From there we rode a bus to Osan Air Force base. The South Koreans manufactured dozens of goods that included the latest women's clothing and shoes, handbags, jewelry, flip phones, grandfather clocks, football and basketball jerseys, suits, sneakers, beautiful paintings, waterfall vases and much more.

If I wanted something specific, I gave the tailor a picture, and they would make it. The prices were reasonable and negotiable. Quanta also had an opportunity to go to an Army Ball. This was a formal night where we celebrated being in the Army. We looked nice and the food was great. I won a bicycle in a raffle drawing, and we had fun.

Camp Market South Korea

US Army Ball

CHAPTER 29

Yongsan, South Korea

After a month, Quanta flew back to the states, and since that was my sixth month in the country, I emailed my career manager. I expressed my interest in an assignment at Fort Jackson. He emailed me back and said he would try. Due to personnel shortages, I transferred from Camp Market to Yongsan main post. I now work at the main post office and served as the Custodian of Postal Effects (COPE). My primary job was to train soldiers to become window clerks. I issued stamps, money orders, and cash daily. Additionally, I inspected unit mail rooms for compliance. Because the main post office was a location where our truck drivers from Kimpo Airport dropped off mail, I already knew my soldiers and they were sharp. I lived in a barracks far away from my soldiers and only for sergeants. I had my own room, and the showers and urinals were down the hallway. After physical training, I returned to my barracks. I walked down the hallway, and a Marine exited his room. He nodded, opened our ice machine door, grabbed a Budweiser, and started chugging. It was 0730 hours; therefore, I knew not to drink with him.

Once I learned my job, I volunteered to take a one week forty-hour bus driving course. It was the size of a transit bus and a five speed. I drove slowly around the post, and it was easy. However, once I drove outside the gates, there were dozens of people standing at crosswalks and bumper to bumper traffic. I drove slowly. Once the traffic began to flow, I drove the speed limit. When I drove down narrow twisting roads separated by concrete dividers, I scrapped the sides of the bus. But after driving that route multiple times, I done so error free and completed the course. I also volunteered to take part in our noncommissioned officer (NCO) of the month and quarter boards. At those boards, senior leadership evaluated us on <u>appearance</u>, knowledge of common soldier skills, military programs, and current world events. My soldier and I competed and won them both.

On the weekends, I was in and out of clubs. One night, I staggered into my barracks hungry and sleepy. I walked upstairs and grabbed two turkey burgers. Then I walked downstairs to our full kitchen. I seasoned my burgers and put them in the pan. Since they were frozen and I was drunk and tired, I walked back to my room to wait. I was awakened by loud knocking. I said, "Oh sh$$!," because I remembered the burgers and I had no idea how long I had been sleeping. My neighbor said that the fire department was downstairs, and they needed everyone to exit the barracks. It was after 0130 hours, and I heard people talking about someone leaving unattended food on the stove. They did not know it was me, but when I did it again, they found out it was me and they began to call me Mr. Burn Man.

Although I did drink alcohol, I done physical training daily. The hills in Yongsan were very steep and I had great stamina. My soldier's physical conditioning, job knowledge, and work ethics were also on point. Those positive attributes overshadowed my excessive drinking. One Saturday night, it was well after midnight, and I was walking back to my barracks from the club when I saw a man walking towards me from about forty yards on the opposite side of the street. I recognized the walk, and I knew that it was my first sergeant.

He had been drinking and was on his way to my barracks to find me. The military police had called him and said that there was an unlocked door at the post office. I had the keys in my room, He fussed at me, and it never happened again.

My unit planned a trip to the N Seoul Tower. This tower looked like a needle and could be seen from miles away. When we entered, we rode the elevator to the top and walked into the restaurant, but before we sat down, we walked around. The restaurant showed a three-hundred-and-sixty-degree view of Seoul. It was beautiful. The food was good, and we had a great evening. Several weeks later, I was on assignment to Fort Jackson. My unit approved me thirty days of leave and I flew back home in November of 1999.

NCO of the Quarter Award

CHAPTER 30

Fort Jackson, South Carolina

In December of 1999, I returned to the United States, and I was so happy to see Quanta and be back home. I spent plenty of time with family and friends. After paying several fines and acquiring the correct insurance, Quanta and I drove to Fort Jackson, South Carolina and checked into a hotel. The next morning, I signed in at the reception station, and they assigned me to HHC, 24th Infantry Division (Fwd.); however, the main body was at Fort Riley, Kansas. I drove over to my unit and noticed that we worked out of a large trailer. I walked in, stood at parade rest, and spoke to a sergeant first class. He then walked me into an office to meet my supervisor, SFC Strawberry. I introduced myself and we walked into a small conference room to talk. We were a team of twenty soldiers, that also included a one star general. SFC Strawberry asked me, "Where I was from?" and I replied, "Portsmouth, Virginia." When he told me he was too, I almost lost my mind. I thought that was the coolest thing ever. As the day went on, I observed SFC Strawberry. He was a laid back easy-going very articulate professional. He had been in the Army for over twenty-three years and had a cool way of speaking and dealing with people. I was a young sergeant, and the most junior soldier in my unit. I drove home and told Quanta all about my new unit and my supervisor. She was happy for me and that we found an apartment twenty minutes away from Fort Jackson; however, once housing became available, we moved on post. Our housing was only five minutes from my supervisor, so we brought our families together, and our wives became friends. In fact, they talked every day, and the connection that we made was a blessing.

On the job, we done physical training on our own. Since that was the case, I slept in and reported to work at 0830 hours. My workload was light. I processed a document or two, and since the post office was walking distance from where I worked, I picked up the mail every day. If the office phone rang, I passed it to a staff sergeant or my supervisor, and if the general's secretary had a day off, I would fill in by answering the phone. During my lunchtime, I drove Quanta to work at *The Shoe Department* inside the Columbia mall. Everything was going well, and I loved it, but the only downside was that I lacked discipline, and I knew it. The unit was to relax for me.

One four-day weekend, my brother and five of my friends (Red Foxx, Midnight, Bernard, Brian, and Jamal) drove down to Fort Jackson to visit. As soon as they pulled up, Jamal began joking on a guy I worked with *Staff Sergeant Boston* (SSG). We partied in the local area, and it was constant fun. On another occasion, my brother and my friends drove back to Fort Jackson, and this time we drove to Atlanta, Georgia and partied for two days. There was also a time when I received a call from Fat Skyler from JDUB. He was driving with Larry Singleton from Portsmouth to somewhere in Georgia and would be passing through South Carolina. He wanted to stop by and see Quanta and I. It was good to see them.

One day after work, I drove to the mall to pick up Quanta, and on the way home, she complained about not feeling well. When we arrived home, I checked the mail, and we walked inside our apartment. Quanta had decided to take a pregnancy test, and it showed a positive reading. We were happy about the results, and while Quanta was on the phone telling her mom the exciting news, I was reading my mail from the Department of Motor Vehicles (DMV). Since I had not kept the court ordered SR-22 insurance coverage, the DMV had suspended my license. I never told anyone and continued to drive.

CHAPTER 31

Fort Riley, Kansas/ Georgia State Police

My job required me to travel, and the first place I drove to was Fort Gordon, Georgia. It was an hour drive, where I trained for two days and did not learn a thing. I also flew to Kansas City International Airport and drove over two hours to Fort Riley, Kansas. I signed for a barracks room, and I reported to our training site. This time around the training was better. After work, I drove around the post, and I was so glad I was not stationed there. There were military police officers and infantry soldiers everywhere. When I drove off the post, the immediate area surrounding the post reminded me of the 1970's television show *Little House on the Prairie*.

Wednesday morning, I had an early morning flight. I checked out of my room around 0400 hours, and since it was dark outside and I did not know the area, I drove very slowly. Thirty minutes into my drive, I saw a police car approaching on the opposite side of the road. I thought to myself I had nothing to worry about. Up until that point, everywhere I drove, I done the speed limit. If I changed lanes, I used my signal lights. I also came to a complete stop before pulling off. As we passed each other, I looked in my rear-view mirror and I imagined the police officer done the same thing; because I saw the police officer make a U-turn and cut on his lights. I remembered saying to myself that I had done nothing wrong and wondered why he was pulling me over. He asked for my license and registration, and I gave it to him. I also gave him my military identification card. The police officer told me that he had stopped me because of a faulty taillight. I explained to him that I was driving a rental car, and it was not my fault. However, he then walked back to his car to see whether my driver's license was valid. He walked back to my car and said that the DMV had revoked my license. He placed me in handcuffs, told me that I was under arrest for driving on a suspended license and drove me to the police station.

When I entered the police station, an officer told me to take that off in here. His tone was very nasty tone, and he was referring to my do rag. When I looked around, I noticed that I was the only Black person in the building, so I answered their questions, and they placed me in a clear glass room. I sat there for hours until they finally allowed me to bail myself out. I do not remember how I found my way back to my rental car, but once I did, I called my supervisor, and he already knew about my incident. I drove to the airport and returned to Fort Jackson. Upon my return, SFC Strawberry counseled me in writing, and I also had to pay fines and keep my court ordered SR-22 insurance. I believed that my senior leadership wanted to severely punish me, but I also believed that SFC Strawberry had something to do with that not happening. I complied and continued to travel.

While Quanta was not happy with my poor decision making, her pregnancy was going well. I was glad because I had to leave again for training. This time SFC Strawberry and I had training in Atlanta, and for two days we trained, stayed in a nice hotel, and ate well. At night, I stayed in my room, drank beer, and watched television. I chilled out because I was with my supervisor. I drove there and back without anything bad happening.

A few weeks later, Staff Sergeant Boston and I had training at Fort Stewart Georgia. We left early that morning. I drove my car and he rode with me. Since I felt he was there to supervisor me, I did not speed. An hour and a half into our drive, we were somewhere in Georgia, on a two-lane interstate, and since there was no traffic, I rode in the left-hand lane. I looked into my rearview mirror, and there was only one car behind me. It was forty yards away. Without turning on my right signal light, I moved over into the right lane. I done this intentionally, but moments later, I saw police lights and a car heading my way. I told Staff Sergeant Boston that the police were behind another car and us. I told him this just as a courtesy. Plus, I believed that I had nothing to be worried about. My license was valid, I was not speeding, and another car was behind me. I knew the police officer was after that car not me. However, once the police car passed the only car behind me, I was the only other vehicle on the road. I looked at the staff sergeant and said, "Man this is some bullsh$$!" He told me to relax. The police officer drove behind me and I pulled over. I rolled down my window and handed him my license and registration. He asked me, "If I knew why he had pulled me over?" and I replied, "No sir." He said, "It was because I did not use my right signal light prior to moving over." He then asked me, "Where we were going?" I said we were active-duty soldiers headed to Fort Stewart for training. He checked my license and since there were no issues, he gave me a warning and allowed us to leave.

I continued driving and we made it to our hotel. Once I checked into my room, I sat on my bed still puzzled as to how that police officer saw us. I knew that he was not in my line of site, and I believed that he could not have seen me either. So, I logged onto my laptop and read about Georgia's traffic laws. I found that by law Georgia had the right to watch traffic via aerial view; in fact, they had an elaborate traffic camera network. The view from the cameras was well enough to see the license plate, and anyone sitting in the front seat of a vehicle.

The next day, it was hot. We trained in and out of trailers, and when the day was over, I was happy. Staff Sergeant Boston knew of a nice club and asked if I wanted to go. I said of course. That evening we sat in my room, drank beer and Bombay Gin, and watched television. Afterwards, we called a taxi and rode to the club. The club was small and packed full of people. I did not buy a drink and I did not need too. I was drunk, tired, and knew we had to work in the morning. The next day was another hot one at work. I smelled like a bottle of liquor. After work, I called Quanta, ate fast food, and fell asleep. We returned to Fort Jackson without any drama, and I was relieved.

When I drove to work the next day, my supervisor told me I had to take a physical training test soon. I began exercising but continued eating and drinking whatever I wanted. On test day, I failed my physical training test, and was overweight. The unit restricted me of any possibilities for favorable actions until I met the standards.

CHAPTER 32

Success & Failure

One weekend, Specialist Hernandez a soldier I had in South Korea drove from Fort Lee to visit Quanta and me. We were happy to see him, and that evening I suggested that he and I go out to eat. Since Quanta was close to her due date, I did not go too far away. Later that night, Quanta called me and said she was going into labor. I told her to call the ambulance and that I was on the way. When I arrived home, Quanta was already in the back of the ambulance. It drove off and I followed it to the hospital. While we were in the delivery room, Quanta laid there in pain, and I sat beside her until it was time for her to deliver. I remained in the room with her and watched the birth of my first child. It was cool and sickening at the same time. Afterwards, I watched the doctor examine our baby, and I noticed that when the doctor raised one of her arms, it fell as if it had no feeling. I was concerned but I did not say anything to Quanta, because I wanted to make sure that she was OKAY, and I did not want to tell her anything upsetting. The doctor and nurses continued their checks and cleaned our baby. Jaylin Aude Hicks was born on September 16, 2000. As Quanta laid there holding Jaylin, the doctor informed us that he had damaged the nerves in her right arm. He diagnosed Jaylin with brachial plexus, and we were upset.

My unit gave us a baby shower. It was nice and we appreciated it. Jaylin now had to begin therapy and it was once a week every week. Jaylin was a beautiful baby and quickly became my everything. I held her all the time. We played and I never let her cry. If she woke up at night, I proudly held her until she fell back to sleep. As Jaylin grew older, when she woke up, I laid her on my chest. If that did not work, I carried her into our front room. Then I turned our stereo on low and played a song called *The Whole World*. It was written by a hip-hop group called Outcast. I held her in my left arm and laid her head on my shoulder. Jaylin's face was facing me, and I could see her pretty eyes in the dark. After kissing her a dozen times, I gently rocked and danced to the song, and I believed that Jaylin enjoyed this as well.

SFC Strawberry transferred, and I got a new supervisor, who was also a sergeant first class that had served as a drill sergeant before arriving to our unit. This meant that there was no more sleeping in for me and for weeks I had to do physical training with him every morning. I lost weight and I passed my physical training test. Since I had passed, I asked my supervisor if I could go to The Basic Non-commissioned Officer Course (BNCOC). The BNCOC course was offered at Fort Jackson, one hundred yards from where I worked. If I planned to earn staff sergeant, it was a course I had to complete. My supervisor was fine with it, but as he contemplated how to sell this idea to our senior leadership, he told me to continue exercising and I did.

After he spoke with our leadership, they did not want to send me. I did pass my physical training test, but I barely passed my height and weight. If I failed my height and weight at school, it would be an embarrassment to myself and the unit. I assured them all I would pass. They reconsidered and decided to send me. The day before I reported to school, my unit checked my height and weight and I barely passed. But I did pass, so the next morning, I reported to the school at 0400 hours. The first thing the instructors done was check for height and weight compliance. The sergeant measured me, and I had exceeded the standards. I was then measured two more times by two different instructors. I failed both and I was dropped from the course. My senior leadership was mad, but I did not become discouraged. I continued exercising and was able to quickly meet the standards once again.

One day, while I was bored at work, I decided to call the Army's automated system to see whether I was on assignment. I had no reason to be, but when I called, I was on assignment to the United States Army Recruiter School. I did not believe it, but it was true. I called the Department of the Army and made excuses for not being able to recruit but it did not work and two months later, I reported to school, passed my physical fitness test, and met my height and weight standards. The recruiting course was a six-week course given at Fort Jackson. It taught me all about the various Army programs, jobs, and incentives that the Army offered. I also learned how to conduct telephone and face to face interviews. The most challenging part of the course was when we drove off post to the mall and practiced talking to people about the Army. This was a challenge for me because I was an introvert. In addition, recruiting was hard work and incredibly stressful. While in school, I asked to recruit in Portsmouth but was denied; however, two weeks before graduation, the Army told me that I would recruit in Charlottesville, Virginia. The movers packed our belongings and placed everything in storage, and on July 13, 2002, we moved back to Virginia.

Jaylin Hicks

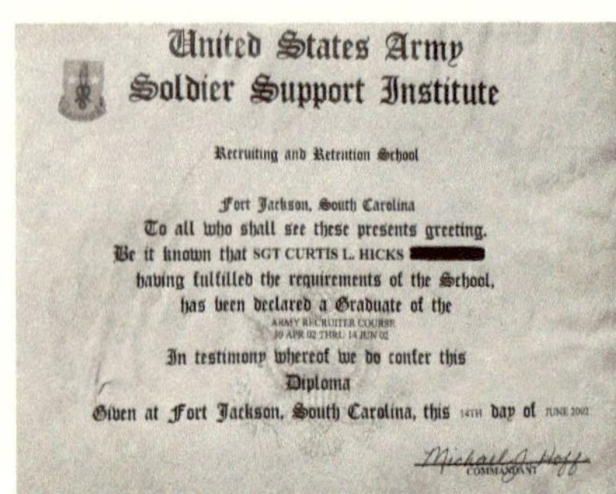

US Army Recruiter School

CHAPTER 33

Charlottesville Recruiting Station

Quanta and I visited friends and family in Portsmouth for thirty days while I was on leave. I had to report to Charlottesville on a Monday, so that Sunday I drove two-and-a-half hours alone, while Quanta and Jaylin stayed with my mother-in-law. When I arrived, I noticed how clean the city looked as I drove to the recruiting station which was a small building located next door to Gold's Gym. The main attraction in the city was the University of Virginia (UVA), which was also where the United States Army's Judge Advocate General (JAG) School was located. After reconning the area, I checked into a hotel and reported to work at 0830 hours the next morning. My supervisor was a staff sergeant from Georgia, and although I had no proof, I felt as if he was a racist. I also worked with two other recruiters. We shared the building with the Marines, Air Force, and Navy recruiters, and they were all White. My supervisor told me that I had to report to our company headquarters which was an hour and twenty minutes away in Richmond, Virginia to in process into the company. On my way out the door, I saw a Black

Marine recruiter. We spoke, and I noticed how stressed he looked. When I arrived at the company headquarters, I met my commander who was a redneck infantry soldier. I immediately had a bad feeling about him, and when he asked me where I was from, I replied, "Norfolk, Virginia." When I was introduced to my first sergeant, who was Black, we looked at each other and smiled. He had been the supervisor of the Portsmouth recruiting station when I joined the Army. He knew me well. It was good to see a familiar face in him.

My unit gave me ten days off to find a place to live, so I drove back to Portsmouth to get Quanta and Jaylin and we found a nice apartment within the city. After that it was time to start recruiting. I reported to the recruiting station at 0830 hours. My supervisor told me that Charlottesville and Albemarle High Schools were my responsibility. He handed me a phone roster and I began making calls to recent college graduates. Afterwards, he drove me to meet high school, college, courthouse, and police department administrators. That evening, another recruiter and I drove to our local mall to recruit, and I talked to anyone that looked qualified.

The first week I focused on filling out and executing whatever I wrote down in my planning guide. After my morning phone calls, I drove to both high schools to set up booths in the cafeteria. I also met with some of the teachers especially those that were veterans, to gain the trust of everyone. Later that afternoon, I visited the Charlottesville-Albemarle Technical College and done the same things, before driving over to the University of Virginia's campus. I quickly learned that those students were not interested in joining the military, so I spent more time in the community. Wherever people were gathered, I was there too, and I rarely met anyone ignorant. However, the city was small, and so was my area of responsibility. One day I asked my supervisor about the outlining areas. He looked at another recruiter, smiled and said that "I could not go out there," and I knew exactly what he meant.

Within a month of being on recruiter duty, I sent my first sergeant an email telling him that I felt that my coworkers and the community were not receptive of me. He called my cell phone, and I went into detail explaining more of what had transpired over the past month. After I finished speaking, he asked me, "If I had a problem with White people?" I said, "No first sergeant." He then began to tell me about a previous Black recruiter that had experienced success in Charlottesville years prior. He then questioned why I told the commander I was from Norfolk and not Portsmouth and told me to get it together before hanging up the phone. This conversation really bothered me. I wondered why if I was the one who was having the issue with racism, why would he ask me if I liked White people? I also had an inclination that he did not believe me, and that he was making it more about me not wanting to recruit in Charlottesville than paying attention to my allegations. So, I emailed him again and told him that I was not a racist, and furthermore, if I met a soldier from Hampton, Virginia and I said Portsmouth, they knew exactly what I was talking about. Our commander was from the bowels of Georgia. I knew that he had heard of Norfolk, Virginia because there were Interstate 64 East signs everywhere in Richmond. My first sergeant never responded.

CHAPTER 34

First Nine Months

My first nine months in recruiting were probationary. If I were substandard, they could send me back to the regular Army, but that was not going to happen because unless it was medically related, soldiers remained on recruiting duty until their tours ended. Normally, the new recruiters trained with a more experienced recruiter, and the first person charged with that responsibility was my supervisor; however, he only recruited with me for a total of three hours. I really did not care because it allowed me to do whatever I wanted to, and after making my morning phone calls, I filled my tank full of gas and went to visit my high schools. Afterwards, I drove in and out of shopping centers looking for recruits, and when I got tired, I drove home and took a nap. I had the house to myself because Quanta was working at the UVA Bookstore and Jaylin was in daycare.

To join the Army, an applicant had to pass a physical and the Armed Services Vocational Aptitude Battery (ASVAB) test. The MEPS in Richmond administered the test, and every week a test administrator drove from Richmond to the Charlottesville National Guard Armory to administer the test. There were two types of applicants and their scores on the ASVAB determined if they were considered a quality or non-quality applicant. An applicant had to score between thirty-one and ninety-nine to be eligible for enlistment. The applicants that scored between a thirty-one to forty-nine were a non-quality applicant, and those applicants that scored between a fifty to ninety-nine were a quality applicant. Quality applicants counted towards our station's monthly mission, and although the non-quality applicants (e.g., low test score, non-high school graduate) could join the Army, they did not count towards our mission. For me to meet my monthly quota, I had to put two quality people in the Army every month.

During my first two months as a recruiter, I did not put anyone in the Army and this was known in the recruiting world as "rolling a donut," which was alarming to those who checked recruiter production. Therefore, I had to attend what was referred to as "zero roller training" during the first week of my third month in recruiting. I was required to put on my Army dress uniform and drive two and a half hours to Beckley, West Virginia. I met with the battalion's training sergeant and other recruiters that were also there for training. We trained for hours. I then drove back to my recruiting station, picked up another recruiter, drove to the mall, and spent the rest of the evening recruiting.

Finally on one Tuesday night, I had an applicant who had scored over fifty on the ASVAB test to commit to joining the Army. On test nights, I worked until 2130 hours even though I had to be up at 0330 hours to drive to my applicant's house to pick him up and take him to Richmond to the MEPS. Before my applicant could enlist, he had to take and pass a drug test and a physical. Then he could select a job. After completing all these requirements my applicant joined the Army later that afternoon. I only put one person in the Army that month, and it felt better than rolling a donut, but unfortunately, the victory was short lived, because it was the end of the month and the beginning of a new recruiting month.

The next month, I screwed around the entire month and rolled another donut, but this time when I drove to Beckley, West Virginia, I had to meet with my battalion sergeant major. He called me into his office, cursed me out and told me that I was collecting a free paycheck. He also told me that if I did not produce, he would have my rank demoted to corporal. I attended more training with our battalion training sergeant and returned to Charlottesville. I tried to compare myself with the other new recruiter that was in our office. He was a promotable combat arms staff sergeant that arrived two months before I did, and he was also good friends with our supervisor and company commander. When people called our office ready to join the Army, the recruiter did not have to work hard to convince them to enlist. These were the calls that my supervisor never gave me as a lead. They were always given to his two other recruiters. Now, I am not saying that the staff sergeant did not work, but after his first year, he was one of the top recruiters in our battalion.

CHAPTER 35

Racism

As a recruiting station, we were required to attend quarterly training in Richmond with all the recruiters in our company. One day at training, a recruiter from Richmond asked me, "How I was doing?," I said that "I was all right." Then he asked me, "How was I able to collaborate with my supervisor?" The Richmond recruiter had spoken with my supervisor on a few occasions, and he also felt as if he was a racist. He also stated that the other new recruiter that I worked with was arrogant.

Later that morning after training, we all drove to separate shopping centers in Richmond to look for recruits. While doing this, I spoke with someone that was interested, so I wrote down their information. When we returned to Charlottesville, I told my supervisor about the lead that I had from Richmond. He told me to work it and I did. A few days later, the supervisor from one of the Richmond recruiting stations called my supervisor and said that the applicant that I contacted was already collaborating with one of his recruiters. He also said that "I did not have the authority to recruit in their area, and that before we drove back from Richmond, I should have given that information to someone in a Richmond recruiting station." After they hung up, the sergeant who worked in that area called our office and chewed me out. As I sat on the phone listening, my supervisor stood close by listening and laughing, and I could sense that he enjoyed hearing two Black recruiters engage in conflict. I hung up, stepped outside, sat in my recruiter car, and called the recruiter and his supervisor back to apologized and explained what happened. They accepted my apology and felt sorry for me because they knew that I was working for a racist. They recommended that I be careful.

Since Quanta and I only had one car, my supervisor allowed me to drive my recruiter car home. On my way home, I began to stop by the bar and if I did not go to the bar, I would stop by a gas station for beer. I continued doing just enough to get through the day; however, one day I stopped by the barbershop to get a haircut and post business cards. As I stared out the window, I saw a man that resembled a childhood friend of mines. So, I called out his name, Gerald Morgan, and it was him. I was happy to see him. We exchanged numbers, and a month later we connected. He came to my apartment and met my family. We watched television, drank beer, and reminisced about JDUB. After work, we began to meet at local bars for drinks, and eventually I met people that he knew, and we all partied. We done the same thing on the weekends, but while I was out having fun, Quanta was becoming tired of my behavior. So, instead of continuing to argue with Quanta, I moved out, rented an apartment, and became roommates with Morgan.

The very first night that we moved into our apartment, the neighbors complained to the rental office about our loud music. We continued to drink alcohol every day. In fact, one night, I got so drunk that I could not report to work the next morning, and over the next three months, I gained weight and developed a gut. When it was time to take my physical fitness test, I failed the run and my height and weight check. Therefore, another recruiter and I from our office had to do physical fitness training with our supervisor. He lived thirty minutes away from me and we had to drive to his house every morning. When I arrived, the area was hilly and wooded. It was also in the same area that I could not recruit because of my skin *color*. I done this Monday through Friday, and every month I also had to drive to our headquarters in Richmond so that the training sergeant could check my height and weight. I eventually passed my physical training test, and met the standards, so I began exercising on my own and was able to stop driving to my supervisor's house.

By now I had been recruiting for over fourteen months. My first sergeant had completed his tour of duty and was no longer in our unit. Now it was my supervisor's last day in recruiting, and I was thrilled. That evening, since he was leaving, the promotable staff sergeant suggested we all have dinner next door to our recruiting station. I did not know why he wanted to do this because our supervisor was not in the building, but I agreed to go. The staff sergeant ordered an alcoholic beverage, so I ordered a beer. This was the first time I had a beer around anyone at work. As I sat there quietly, the other two recruiters conversated. I was not listening to what they were talking about, until a few moments later when the promotable staff sergeant looked at me, and said with a smile that, "I was the first Black person our supervisor ever liked." I looked at them, shook my head, walked out the restaurant and drove to a bar.

I thought about reporting the incident, but if I reported it, the investigators would interview my supervisor, commander, first sergeant, and the other two recruiters that I worked with, and this would cause problems within our station. I also knew that if I spoke to an investigator and mentioned the *Richmond incident*, it would involve other recruiters when they needed to be recruiting, and if the investigators spoke to my battalion sergeant major, who knew me from zero roller training, he would not support me. I felt it was worthless and I let it go. I later found out that the promotable staff sergeant was now my new supervisor until a replacement arrived.

We continued to work Monday through Saturday, and when I did not work on Saturdays, my friends from Portsmouth would visit me and Morgan. We had fun showing them around town, and on the Saturdays when I wanted to go home, I filled up my recruiter car with my government credit card, bought a six pack of beer, and Morgan and I drove to Portsmouth.

Our recruiting headquarters finally sent us a new supervisor, who was a sergeant first class, and his background was combat arms. We all knew him from our Richmond training sessions, and he was also great friends with the company commander and everyone I worked with. As a recruiting station, we began to do physical fitness every morning, and after my morning phone calls, I continued to recruit. One evening, while I was in the office sitting at my desk, I saw police lights flashing. So, I walked outside, and saw that the police lights were affixed to the inside of my supervisor's personal car. He told me that he was affiliated with the local law enforcement and trained officers in tactical operations. After learning that, I knew I had to slow down.

CHAPTER 36

The Movie Major Payne & Washington Redskins

A few weeks later, I was walking out of our recruiting station and overheard the Marines talking about a private school in our area. They said that it was off limits because a recruiter had done something wrong years ago. I knew that I needed to figure out which school they were referring to, so I checked the internet and learned it was a co-educational private preparatory school named *The Miller School of Albemarle.*

I emailed the school to see if I could schedule a meeting regarding the possibility of me recruiting on their campus. I received a positive response in which they agreed to meet with me, and I was beyond excited. I drove over to the campus, which was nice and clean, and walked up the long flight of steps to the main office. I introduced myself to the administrators. Everyone was genuinely nice, professional, and well spoken. We then walked into a conference room and discussed their past concerns with recruiters, and I understood why they had placed the ban on recruiters in their school. However, they did reconsider and decided to allow only me to recruit once a week on Thursday afternoons on their campus. At the conclusion of our meeting, I thanked them, and a staff member gave me a tour of the campus. As we walked through the hallways, I could see that the classrooms were full of students. We then exited the building and walked to the back of the school. The administrator asked me, "If I had saw the movie *Major Payne?*" and I replied, "Yes." The administrator then told me that we were standing on that same field that the scene where Major Payne told his cadets to meet him on the field to introduce himself was filmed. Later in the movie, Major Payne made his cadets wear dresses and run around the campus. When the cadets ran in front of the school, the movie showed a large building with steep steps to climb. Those were the steps I climbed to enter the building.

Since there were no other recruiters allowed on campus, I felt as if I had struck gold. I knew any of their students could max our ASVAB test. On my first visit to the school, I wanted to show my face and say hello to every student and staff member I saw, and with each visit, the goal was to build trust and rapport. I spoke with students, and honestly most were not interested; because they had goals of being accepted into a prestigious college. However, an administrator introduced me to a student, who was a senior, appeared to be in excellent shape, and was interested in the Army Special Forces. One day after school, I drove my applicant to our recruiter station. Normally, when I met an applicant that was interested in something combat arms related, I would introduce them to another recruiter in our office, so that they could talk the lingo. After speaking with my supervisor, he agreed to only taking the ASVAB test. So, on test night, I picked him up from school and we drove to the testing site. On our way there he told me that he was from the Northern Virginia area, and I told him I was from Portsmouth. When we arrived, we walked into the testing center, checked in, and then I waited in my car. Two hours later, my applicant was finished and scored a ninety-nine.

A month later, he enlisted into the Army for four years as a Special Forces soldier and received a large bonus. He was happy and scheduled to leave for basic training after high school. We met weekly and everything was going well until an incident occurred that required him to appear in court. On the day of his court appearance, his dad wanted me to be there, and I agreed to come. I drove to northern Virginia and met them at the courthouse. His dad was well dressed and looked like a businessman. We shook hands, walked into the courtroom, and sat down. The judge called my recruit to the stand and explained to him why he was there, but once the judge learned of him joining the Army, he dropped the charges and made him pay a fine. Afterwards, we walked outside of the courtroom. We were all happy and relieved. His dad then asked me, "If I was a football fan?" and I said, "Yes, I like the Washington Redskins." Turns out that he was a Redskins season ticket holder. He asked for my mailing address and said that he would send me some tickets. I was very appreciative and thanked him, and a few days later, he mailed me four front row tickets to see the Washington Redskins verses the Minnesota Vikings. I was amped.

The night before the game, Morgan, Cameron, and I drove to northern Virginia to Staff Sergeant Warren's house and that night, we partied in DC and had fun. The next morning, we drove forty-five minutes through dense traffic to the stadium. When we arrived and parked, there were Redskins fans everywhere. We saw people grilling food, drinking beer, and I loved the environment. We entered the stadium and walked down to the first row. As we stood there looking at the field, Warren saw Joe Nathan walking on the field. We yelled his name, and he acknowledged us by raising his hand. There was also a teenage boy walking on the field, so Warren called him over and asked if he would get Joe Nathan to sign his football. Warren agreed to pay him twenty dollars and the boy got Joe to sign Warren's football. We were the only people sitting on the front row, and the curious people around us began asking us who we were. We told them we were in the Army. When I stopped the man that was selling hotdogs and asked him, "How much they were?" He said, "Everything was free." I ate at least six hotdogs, had a great time and we all returned home safely.

I also had a recruit whose family worked for Delta Airlines, that I asked about a hook up on a flight to Miami. He said sure, so I reached out to Gilbert who was from Florida and lived close to the beach. I only paid eighty-nine dollars for a round trip ticket, and it was worth every penny. Miami was fun. We stayed out all night, drinking alcohol and hanging out in clubs. We also drove to Homestead, Florida and toured *The Everglades National Park*. They offered at least three types of admissions, so we chose the general admission which included a walking tour through a dozen alligator farms. There were hundreds of alligators of all sizes. We also sat and watched a snake and alligator show. After the show, I needed a beer and was ready to leave, besides that place was creepy. So, we drove back to Miami and partied some more.

The next day, my flight was due to fly out at noon. As I walked through the airport terminal, I looked through a crowded seating area and saw a man that resembled Dennis Green, who was successful Black NFL head coach. I stopped walking and looked again just as he looked up and smiled. I could not believe it was really him. So, I went and bought a portable camera, walked over to him without making a scene, and asked if we could take a picture together? I was so happy when he agreed. I returned to Charlottesville feeling rejuvenated.

CHAPTER 37

My Last Days

The week after I returned, I visited a math class at Charlottesville High School to speak with a group of twelfth graders. When I walked in, I noticed that the teacher had basic math problems on the board (e.g., 4x4 or 8x7). This was alarming to me and a signal that something was wrong. I spoke to the class and there were two students who were interested in joining the Army; however, I told the teacher that I did not believe his students would pass the ASVAB test. He informed me that his students had never learned math, and for years their teachers just pushed them through the system. He also stated that if his students showed up, tried, and were not disruptive, he passed them with a D. Eighty percent of these students were Black, and not only did I feel sick to my stomach, but I also felt sorry for those students. I shared my experience with Quanta, and we promised to never allow this to happen to Jaylin.

With only eight months to go before my tour ended, the Army was experiencing a shortage of recruiters, which cause some recruiters to be involuntarily extended beyond their original end of tour dates. I did not want that to happen to me, so I emailed my career manager and asked about attending BNCOC. My career manager requested that I call him, which I did and after our conversation, he helped me get a school date.

In recruiting, the mission was first, and our leadership did not like to send anyone to school. So, I knew that once my leadership found out about my school date, they would be mad and may try to postpone it.

Well to my surprise, one day, my supervisor spoke to me about my BNCOC class date, and he was fine with it. In fact, he wanted to help me with my physical fitness and height and weight check. Since I had a confirmed school date, I had to drive to Richmond monthly to have my height and weight checked, and just like before, I always barely passed. I wondered why he wanted to help me; however, I knew that it was possible for me to fail my height and weight check at school again, so I said, "Ok," and took the help. After work, he told me to change into my physical fitness training uniform, pack my rucksack, and report back to the recruiting station at 2000 hours, because we were going on a road march. We began at our recruiting station and quickly reached a wooded area that I had never thought of walking through. We spent four hours walking through the woods. Once we returned to our recruiting station, I did an excessive amount of physical training inside our office. This included log lifting and dips. Around 0345 hours, I was exhausted, and he finally released me. I thanked him, and as I walked outside to my car, my supervisor walked out and said "Sergeant Hicks, you owe me. If you pass your height and weight, I want you to take out those gold teeth." I said to myself, "This mother$$$$$$ is another racist!," but aloud I said," Hooah, Sergeant" and drove off. As I drove to my apartment, I felt as if my commander had something to do with this as well, but either way, I was not taking out my gold teeth.

The next morning, I told Quanta about the incident from the previous night while I packed my bags. I never asked or needed his help, and only I knew that I had been to BNCOC before and failed a height and weight test. This would be a paid vacation with per diem, and I was not going to drive for six hours, fail and return to recruiting. In recruiting, whenever we had an applicant that could barely pass their height and weight test, we applied icy hot around their stomach and tightly wrapped that area with *Saran Wrap*. Then, we would wrap a black waist band around their stomach to helped them quickly lose water weight and inches around their waist.

Before I left, Quanta wrapped me the same way and this made it an uncomfortable drive to Fort Jackson. When I arrived, I checked into a room on post, ate light, gently laid down in bed, and slept with the wrap on. The next morning, I woke up around 0330 hours, used scissors to cut the wrap off, and reported to the school. I easily passed my physical training test, height, and weight, and for the next thirty days, I learned more about my career field. It was fun, challenging, and I met some good people. While I was in school, I thought about recruiting and I hated the thought of returning. I only had seven months left until my tour ended, but I knew that if I kept the same attitude, I was only hurting myself. My attitude was the one thing that I had control over. I completed BNCOC and drove back to Charlottesville, and it felt great to see my family. I drove to my apartment, picked up my personal belongings and moved back home.

When I reported to work, I did not talk to anyone unless someone said something to me. I began making phone calls. Afterwards, I drove to the high schools and scheduled future classroom presentations. I followed up with earlier applicants and talked with a few more people. I continued to do physical training on my own and I talked even less to the people that I worked with. I did not trust anyone. I knew how to recruit and that was what I focused on.

When applicants were interested in joining the Army, I learned why they were interested and focused on it. I also sold our benefits (e.g., free medical, dental, education, bonuses, guaranteed job/

pay, travel). Normally, soldiers did not work on the weekends, and if there was a federal holiday, we were off for four days. We were granted thirty days of leave a year and were off for two weeks during Christmas. It was true, soldiers only worked half a year.

One day as I walked through the Walmart parking lot in Charlottesville, I saw a man in an Army dress uniform. He was an officer. When I walked closer to salute him, we smiled because we knew each other. It was *Captain Thomas formerly known as Sergeant Thomas from Fort Campbell*. He was at UVA to complete a course at the JAG school. I told him I was recruiting. Before he became a commissioned officer, he was also a *warrant officer*. I was quite impressed, and it did not surprise me. He was one of the most **determined** soldiers I had ever met. He even kicked me in the a$$ for just being a *sergeant*. We exchanged numbers and he stopped by our apartment. It was great seeing him.

A few weeks later, I drove to northern Virginia and sat down with my career manager to discuss my next assignment. I told him that I was interested in going to Japan. He looked at me like I was crazy and said, "Germany, Hawaii, Fort Drum New York, and Fort Riley, Kansas were available." I said, "No thank you, and asked about South Korea." It was available. I accepted the assignment, thanked him, and drove back to Charlottesville. I always chose South Korea because it was only a one-year assignment, I would earn more money, and in my fifth month, I could fly home. Quanta understood that both Germany and Hawaii were three-year assignments, and although, she and Jaylin would have been with me, that was too long for me to be away from my brother and friends in P-town.

No one ever spoke to me about extending my time in recruiting, and I was thankful. I continued recruiting and averaged one contract per month. Finally, it was the first day of my last month in recruiting, and my first sergeant called my cell phone to tell me that he needed two contracts from me. The sooner I complied, the sooner I could go home and not have to return. So, the first week, I wrote a contract, and a week later, I drove another applicant to the MEPS to enlist. She was happy and I was too. Afterwards, we drove back to Charlottesville. When we walked into our office, everyone congratulated her, and I posted her picture on the wall before driving her home.

Later that evening, my first sergeant called to congratulate me, and although I still had two more weeks left to recruit, he was sending me home early. I thanked him, and walked into my supervisor's office and told him that the first sergeant said that "I could leave." He looked at me and said, "You ain't going nowhere." It was 2000 hours, and no one else was recruiting. I walked outside and called the first sergeant back and explained to him what had transpired. He said that "He would call my supervisor, and for me to grab my belongings and go home." That was my last night in recruiting, and I completed my tour of duty in August of 2005.

CHAPTER 38

Dongducheon, South Korea (Camp Casey)

While I was on leave, Cameron, Kenzie, and I drove to Washington D.C. for the twentieth Anniversary of the Million Man March. We enjoyed ourselves with thousands of other Black people who were walking, talking, and peacefully listening to the speakers.

Since Quanta decided that she would continue working and Jaylin would remain in daycare, we did not have to pack our household items. I enjoyed my time off and flew back to South Korea for the third time. This time the reception station assigned me to the 509th Personnel Services Battalion, and I worked at the Camp Casey main post office. The post office sat in the same parking lot where I had rolled down the hill years ago. I met my supervisor, who was a female sergeant first class, and I also met my lieutenant. Then I walked to our administrative office to begin in-processing. A sergeant first class introduced herself and welcomed me to our unit. As she looked through my records, she asked me if I wanted to go back to the promotion board. I said, "Yes sergeant," although I found it odd that she asked me that question. She then said that

"She would speak with my supervisor." I thanked her and returned to the post office.

My supervisor told me that I would serve as the Custodian of Postal Effects (COPE). I had successfully fulfilled those duties years ago and was comfortable with the position. She asked me about the promotion board, and I said, "I could do it, because I had competed and won boards in the past, and it was something that I was good at." Since I was familiar with the position, she concurred. This all happened on my first day in the unit, and normally, soldiers had to prove they were deserving before being given the opportunity to appear before the promotion board. I was grateful and determined to show that I was worthy. I lived in the barracks across the street from the post office, Popeyes Chicken, post exchange, commissary, and a local bar. I supervised eight soldiers and worked alongside two female Korean nationals. We worked six days a week and done physical fitness Monday through Friday. After work, I went to the gym.

I had good soldiers and became good friends with one of them, Specialist Bell. He was from Delaware. He was a diligent worker and focused on continuing his education. We would walk to the bar to shoot pool, eat cheese pizza, and drink Long Island iced teas. If we did not work on Saturdays, we caught the bus to Yongsan or OSAN to shop. Within four months, I passed my promotion board and earned the rank of staff sergeant. I could not thank my leadership enough. I also helped Specialist Bell earn the rank of sergeant. During my fifth month, I flew back home and hung out with my family, and when I returned to South Korea, I saw the sergeant first class who asked me about the promotion board. I noticed that she had lost weight and looked great. I asked her how she did it? She said, "She knew a soldier who tried acupuncture on the South Korean market, and that the soldier had lost weight, so she decided to try it." The doctor also prescribed her some weight loss supplements. I was interested, so I asked her for the doctor's location. When I had some free time, I took a taxi to the doctor's office, and I learned about the practice of acupuncture and how penetrating the skin with thin needles helped with chronic pain and other health issues. In addition, if a person needed to lose weight, the doctor would recommend weight loss supplements. So, I agreed to a session. As I laid on my back on a table, the doctor stuck little needles into my arms, legs, and midsection. It did not hurt but it felt awkward as the needles began to vibrate. This procedure lasted for approximately twenty minutes. Afterwards, the doctor wrote me a prescription for weight loss supplements. The following week, I completed another session, but I lost interest and never filled the prescription.

Once I approached my seventh month in the country, I began to look for my next assignment. The Army had made some changes to the way we were notified of our pending assignments. Soldiers could now log into their GOARMY accounts and see that they were being offered three or more assignments to choose from. When I checked my account, I was not interested in any of the choices that were being offered to me. The good thing about this was that the system updated every week or two and would offer different assignments, so when I checked back, I saw that Fort Eustis, Virginia was available. I quickly accepted this assignment and told Quanta the good news, and of course she was happy about it.

Although this was my third tour in Korea, I wanted to have fun and appreciated the experience of being there. So, one evening, the entire post office decided to have dinner at an authentic Korean restaurant. The Korean nationals we worked with planned the entire evening, and when we entered the restaurant, we removed our shoes, and sat on the floor around a long table. The chef served our food in over a dozen small bowls. I filled my plate using chopsticks. The cuisine was mostly vegetable based with small amounts of meat. They did not serve bread, and the most popular vegetable was Kimchi, which is traditional Korean banchan consisting of salted and fermented vegetables. Although everything tasted great, my favorite was the Yaki Mandu (a Korean dumpling filled with ground beef and vegetables), and Bulgogi (thin slices of beef that is marinated in a savory sweet sauce and quickly cooked over a flame) and rice.

I also signed up for a tour of the Demilitarized Zone (DMZ), which was the area where South Korea and North Korea intersected. On the day of my tour, the tour guide directed our attention to the flying North Korean flag. It was enormous and weighed over six hundred pounds. The highlight of my tour was walking on North Korean soil, but to do so, we had to walk into a blue rectangular shaped building, where there was an exceptionally long table facing in front of us. We then slowly walked to the right and alongside the table stood. Straight ahead stood two tall and armed North Korean soldiers, that looked very intimidating, so we stayed as close to the table as possible. After I walked around it, I promptly exited the building. This was a great experience, and a few months later, I successfully completed my tour and returned home in October of 2006. Once I arrived home, I scheduled a date for the movers to pack our household goods and we *settled* down in Williamsburg, Virginia.

DMZ Fence Wire

Camp Casey Postal Plaque

CHAPTER 39

Fort Story, Virginia

A few weeks after our arrival, we learned that Quanta had a friend in Charlottesville that was selling her car, and since I did not know much about cars, we reached out to a good friend of ours who was an active-duty Army mechanic. SFC Evans and his wife were both from Portsmouth, and we had all graduated from Churchland High School. Our families were intertwined, so he rode with me to check it out. The car was a five speed, 1993, white, four door Honda Accord, that was excellent on gas. Upon his suggestion, I purchased the car and was grateful for his help.

In November of 2006, after my leave was over, I reported to the Fort Eustis Reception Station, and they assigned me to the 11th Transportation Battalion at Fort Story, in Virginia Beach. I explained to the reception sergeant that I had signed a lease in Williamsburg, but obviously this did not matter. So, I drove fifty-five-minutes from Fort Eustis to Fort Story to in-process. I met with my supervisor and our soldiers. During this meeting, my supervisor explained to me that our unit was newly established, and that the unit's policies and procedures were not in place. In addition to all of this, we were due to deploy for fifteen months to Iraq. My supervisor had developed a plan for the deployment, that would involve us dividing the office into two teams. Our office had an abundance of soldiers, so he would take a team of soldiers for the first eight months, then, I would deploy with a team to replace them. I agreed with the plan and replied with, "Hooah, Sergeant too easy." Thirty days later, my supervisor and the first wave of soldiers deployed.

I was not prepared for the responsibilities that came with this assignment. Sure, I was a human resource sergeant, but this was my first time overseeing a section, and I also had to set up an office and a unit mailroom. Not to mention that I had spent the past eight years working for a general, doing postal work, and recruiting. So, one day I held a meeting with my soldiers. I told them my background, and explained to them that I needed their help. I felt the best way for me to learn my job was to learn their jobs. I sat down with each soldier and done just that. They were all sharp soldiers, and if I had a question, they either knew the answer or referred to the policy that governed it. Since we had to develop policy letters for everything we processed, I reached out to every Fort Eustis administrative office, and they sent me examples to build from.

I was determined to learn my job and bring us up to standards. This required me to work on most Saturdays. In which I processed paperwork, replied to emails, and personally typed every policy letter we were missing. My soldiers reviewed them multiple times before we went final. Sure, I made mistakes here and there, but we were slowly becoming an office soldiers could rely on to process documents correctly and in a timely manner.

Prior to my arrival, our unit mailroom was under investigation and had been closed. This resulted in the soldiers that lived in the barracks not receiving their mail at all. When I walked over to look at the mailroom, I found that there were hundreds of letters and boxes laying around. In fact, I could not walk through the room without stepping on someone's mail. The soldiers told me that their leadership was having them work the mail, but they had never received the proper training. Obviously, this was unacceptable, so I reached out to the Fort Eustis Main Post Office for guidance. They informed me that, "It had been years since they had trained anyone at Fort Story.," and fortunately, they were aware of our problem and immediately scheduled us a date for training. A few days later, two Fort Eustis Post Office staff members drove to Fort Story and trained our soldiers. After training, my soldiers were evaluated, and they all passed and were certified mailroom clerks. Afterwards, two of my soldiers and I processed all the mail that was in the mailroom. A week later, the inspectors returned to check our mailroom for compliance. We passed and were allowed to reopen our mailroom. My leadership thanked me for my efforts.

Month after month, our office continued to improve, and the soldiers we served began to see how we were processing their documents correctly and in a timely manner. The leadership at Fort Story and Fort Eustis also noticed how well we were doing, and one day my supervisor called our office from Iraq to congratulated us. He also stated that he looked forward to us replacing them. I thanked him before hanging up; however, two months later my supervisor called our office again, but this time he was mad. He told me that, "They had been informed that they would have to complete the whole tour." I told him, "I was sorry to hear that," and we hung up. I kept them all in my prayers for the duration of the tour.

CHAPTER 40

Portsmouth Police Department

Even though the drive to work was long, I enjoyed it. Once I had learned my job, I would drive to Portsmouth on the weekends. My friends and I would meet at Kendrick's house to have fun. Kendrick was in the Navy and an excellent cook, and we had also both grew up in JDUB. We all joked, drank beer, played cards, and played video games for half the night. It did not feel like I was in the Army at all, until one weekend while I was in the Southside area of Portsmouth with Jamal and Goose. We had been drinking beer all day, and I drove to the barbershop at the corner of High Street and Effingham Street where the owner was having a party. We arrived around 1940 hours, and I began taking shots of liquor until around 2100 hours, when I decided to leave because I had become drunk from all of the liquor I had consumed. So, without telling anyone, I walked out the front door to my car which was parked in front of the barbershop. I started the car and drove off, planning to drive to my mother in law's house which was twenty-five minutes away. But halfway into the drive, I realized that I could not make it.

I was at the corner of Portsmouth Boulevard and Shea Street. There was a gas station on the right, and to the left was a church. I made a right and a quick left and parked behind the church, where I then cut my car off, removed my keys from the ignition, and fell asleep.

A few hours later, I heard a knock on the window. It was a police officer flashing his light into my car. I said to myself that this was it. He asked me for my license and registration, before asking me why I was sleeping there. I said, "Sir I had too much to drink, and I could not make it all the way home. The area seemed safe, so I stopped and fell asleep." The police officer walked back to his car to verify my license. He returned and asked me to exit the car. The police officer checked my pockets for weapons and anything illegal, cuffed me, and placed me in his police car. He then proceeded to search my car and when he did not find anything illegal in it, he drove me to the Portsmouth police station.

On the way to the police station, the officer asked me, "How long I had been in the Army?" In a pitiful sounding tone, I said, "Fifteen years, Sir." We arrived and I slept in a holding cell for hours until the arresting officer awakened me. He informed me that, "It was time to go in front of the judge via video teleconference." Before I stepped in front of the camera, the officer said to me, "Since you were polite and did not argue, I am charging you with drunk in public." He also said that "If he were a new police officer, he would have charged me with driving while intoxicated (DWI): because when police officers were new, they did not use their discretion. They charged crimes in accordance with the rule book." I thanked him, the judge fined me and afterwards I was able to leave. I walked up the ramp and down the street to a local taxi stand that was near the corner of County and Chestnut Street, where I took a taxi to my car, and I drove home.

The following Monday morning, I skipped physical training, drove to the Portsmouth courthouse, and paid my fine. I then drove to my work, walked to my first sergeant's office, and told him a story that I made up about me being drunk in a local bar in Portsmouth. I said I was rowdy which resulted in the owner calling the police, and me being charged with public intoxication. I also told him that I had paid the fine and there was nothing else pending. He was not pleased and recommended we waited until we heard from our brigade command sergeant major, who was stationed at Fort Eustis. I said, "Hooah," and walked to my office.

Anytime a soldier was involved in a serious incident off post, the civilian authorities informed the military police, and the military police would produce a blotter report that informed the soldier's brigade commander and brigade command sergeant major of the incident. I knew the supervisor that worked in our brigade command sergeant major's office, so that evening in anticipation of showing up on the blotter report, I called him and talked to him about my incident. I also email him a copy of my fine and money order showing I paid it. The next day the sergeant called me and informed me that, "I was on the report." I anxiously waited to hear from someone in my chain of command, but fortunately, no one ever called. I was so thankful; because, up until that point, my reputation in this unit was flawless. This incident damaged it, but I continued to work hard. Not long after this incident, our office was known as the best in the battalion.

CHAPTER 41

Stomach Problems

I worked long hours and rarely done any physical training; although I could run and do pushups and sit-ups, I could not lose my beer belly. I knew that if my unit checked my height and weight, I would fail, and I could not afford to have that blemish on my records. I had heard about a liposuction office in Virginia Beach, and wanted to learn more, so one day I drove to their office. The lady explained the procedure and how it would target my problem area, which was my stomach. After weighing the pros and cons, I agreed to have it done, but before I walked out of their office, a nurse told me to have someone drive me there on the day of the procedure. I said, "OKAY," but I never said anything to Quanta about it.

On that day, I drove to the office. A nurse walked me into a room, and I changed out of my clothes and into a hospital type garment. I laid on a bed and under sheets with the upper part of my body slightly raised. The nurse placed additional cloths and towels on each side of my bed. Then she placed a heart rate monitor on my finger and called for the surgeon. He sterilized and numbed my entire stomach area, before making two incisions on each side of my stomach. He then connected a tube to one of the incisions, which functioned like a plunger to suck the fat out. I was awake and watched the entire procedure. The fat was white, solid, and looked like the lard cooking shortening. As he finished one incision, he cleaned the area and moved on to the next section. It did not hurt, but it did feel uncomfortable. I do not remember how long the procedure took. However, it was at least two hours.

Before I walked out the door, I swallowed two pain pills that they had given me. I believe that they were narcotics. The nurse asked me, "If I had a driver?," and I told her that, "My driver was outside." The office gave me prescriptions to fill, and I walked out the door; however, I felt tired as soon as I started my car. Even though I had my windows down, I struggled driving home. My heavy eyes opened and closed as I drove over bridges and through the Monitor Merrimac Tunnel. I was fortunate enough to make it to the Farm Fresh grocery store in Williamsburg, where I parked, turned off my car, and passed out. When I woke up, it was 1930 hours and two hours had passed. I drove home, which was five minutes away, and told Quanta what happened. She gave me an ear full and rightfully so.

I was sore but continued to work and during physical training, I walked, and I did not lift anything heavy. I also ate less and drunk less alcohol, and a month after the procedure, I began jogging and playing basketball by myself. My stomach and waist were smaller, and I slowly worked myself back to normal. My unit returned from Iraq, and I was glad to see them, but after a brief conversation with my supervisor, I could tell that he had an attitude. I believed that he was still mad that we did not deploy. Every day at work, the atmosphere was toxic, and his negative attitude towards me was unnecessary. I had nothing to do with his plan backfiring, so I did not communicate with him unless he asked me a question. I stayed out of his way, and in August of 2008, he had me transferred to the 6th Transportation Battalion at Fort Eustis.

CHAPTER 42

Fort Eustis

I drove to the office where I would work at Fort Eustis, and met my new soldiers, and my acting battalion sergeant major. When I walked into his office, he informed me that our battalion was planning to deploy to Iraq for twelve months. The unit had already identified those soldiers who would deploy and that he did not need me to deploy. He also mentioned that he had heard about the positive things that we had done at Fort Story and wanted me to remain in the rear and make his administrative shop the best in the battalion. I said, "Hooah, Sergeant Major to easy." I was so happy, not because I did not have to deploy, but because Quanta and I had found out that we were having another baby.

On my first day, I sat down with my soldiers to introduce myself. They knew of our success at Fort Story, so it was much easier earning their respect. We done physical training Monday through Friday, and after physical training, I quickly showered and drove twenty minutes to work. I began to watch how the office functioned. When the phone rang, I listened to their conversation. I wanted to know if the person calling complained or gave praise. I assessed the soldier's morale, job knowledge, and initiative. They were a good group of soldiers; however, we had two main concerns: our policy letters were outdated, and soldiers were not slotted correctly within our data system. Fortunately for us whatever policy letters we were missing, I had saved on my thumb drive, and with my soldier's help, we quickly became current. I continued working long hours and took work home. I enjoyed what I done, and I was good at it.

I remember talking to the acting battalion sergeant major about going to school; because I needed to complete the Advanced Non-commissioned Officers Course (ANCOC) which was offered at Fort Jackson. I agreed to ensure that my soldiers could maintain our office while I was out. I talked with our unit school's sergeant, and he scheduled me for the thirty-day course with a school date of October 20, 2008. I do not remember anything that I was taught; however, I do remember saving thousands of dollars in per diem, and I exercised daily and watched what I ate. I completed the course on November 25, 2008, and drove back to Fort Eustis.

One day after physical training, my knees were hurting so bad that I had to schedule a doctor's appointment. The doctor told me that I had arthritis and mild degeneration in both knees. It was bad enough to stop me from running; however, I did not want to become a permanent walker. I also did not want my evaluation to reflect that I could not run. So, instead of walking, I scheduled an appointment and opted to have steroids injected into both of my knees. On the day of my first injections, I laid on a table and the doctor's assistant sterilized both of my knees. Suddenly, I saw the doctor pull out a large syringe. When he stuck me, I pulled up on the table and loudly said, "Oh sh$$!" It was so painful that his assistant had to hold me down and as the doctor applied pressure to the syringe, I could feel the thick solution entering my knees. Four days later, the pain was gone, and it felt like I had new knees. After this revelation, I began to drive to my office on Fort Eustis on Saturdays and Sundays and road march between six to eight miles each time.

After I completed my road march, I would go into my office and work. I became an official workaholic.

CHAPTER 43

The Phone Call

When I needed a break, my friends from Portsmouth and I would drive to northern Virginia to visit SSG Tate from Fort Lee. We always had a great time. In addition to these trips, Quanta and I rode a bus twice to New York to shop with family and friends. During one of our trips, while Quanta and I shopped in the Jamaica Colosseum Mall in Queens, I saw Styles P from the hip hop group the LOX, and he looked high as a kite. On another occasion, Jaylin and I rode with Kendrick and his family to Orlando, Florida. This was our first time going to Disney World. The parks were nice. Jaylin enjoyed riding the roller coasters and I enjoyed walking and watching the children have fun. On this trip, I saw the hip hop artist Run from the group Run-D.M.C. We had so much fun.

At work, it was business as usual, until one day, I received word that the Department of the Army planned to release the promotion list for sergeant first class. A friend gave me a call and told me that I had made the list. I was now a promotable staff sergeant. I was incredibly happy and thanked God. Although the promotion was at least eight months down the road, I had never been so motivated to get in shape. Monday through Friday my mornings began at 0400 hours. I would drive to Fort Eustis and jog six to eight miles every morning. After doing this for a month, I began to wake up at 0200 hours and slowly jogged eight to twelve miles a day, and with the help of supplements, I lost thirty-seven pounds in two plus months. I also dropped two uniform sizes, was well under my maximum allowed weight and almost maxed my physical training test.

My soldiers were all in good physical condition and thanks to them, our office was known as the best around. In fact, we never missed a suspense, nor lost or misplaced documents we were given. We also processed everything in a timely manner and maintained accountability of all transactions. I was competitive and being number one meant something to me. It also meant something to my acting sergeant major as well. He was so pleased with our efforts that he presented my soldiers and me with awards.

CHAPTER 44

510th Human Resources Company

After a year in my unit, I transferred to the 510th Human Resources Company. They were a forwarded unit from Fort Bragg and was directly across the street from my current unit. When I walked over, I sat down with my new commander and first sergeant. The plan was for me to deploy; however, they were not sure when, where and in what compacity. My first sergeant made me take charge of a platoon, and every morning we done physical fitness. I spent the rest of my day preparing myself and others for deployment. This included assisting soldiers with setting up power of attorneys, giving custody of children to other family members, putting vehicles in storage, making sure immunizations and examinations were current and up to date, getting married, completing divorces and any other things that the soldiers would need to accomplish prior to deploying.

One day, my battalion sergeant major called me into his office to discuss our battalion's live fire exercise which was quickly approaching. He asked me, "If I could take charge of the exercise." I knew little about running a range, but I said, "Hooah Sergeant Major."

For the next three weeks, I read policies and procedures and solicited help from Fort Eustis range personnel. On the day of our live fire, we formed a convoy of about five vehicles and drove off around 0800 hours. I rode in the front passenger seat of our HUMMV with a young soldier who was my driver. As he drove west on Interstate 64, twenty minutes into the drive, he swerved, and I asked him if he was, OKAY? He said that "He had taken some sleeping pills the night before." I told him to pull over and I drove an hour and a half the rest of the way to Fort A.P. Hill, Virginia. We all arrived safely, and after the captain and I briefed everyone, we began training. Inside of a HUMMV or another military vehicle was the driver, passenger, and two soldiers in the back seat. As the driver drove through a rough terrain driver's range, everyone else practiced firing their M16s out the window at targets, and although hot shell casings fell underneath our collars, we completed our training without any injuries.

A couple of weeks later, I met Lieutenant Baker, who had just arrived from Fort Hood, Texas. After physical training, we walked into our company commander's office, and she informed Lieutenant Baker and I that we would be deploying to Iraq and would serve as the casualty platoon leader and platoon sergeant. She also informed us that she did not know much about our mission, so Lieutenant Baker and I continued to prepare ourselves for deployment. We also learned more about each other. Lieutenant Baker did not have an Army background. He had previously competed for fifteen years around the world as a sprinter, and once retired from the sport he worked at the Pentagon. This was where they offered him an opportunity to serve our country, and once he successfully completed his military obligation, the Pentagon would promote him to a higher position. He accepted their offer and enlisted into the Army as a human resources specialist. After training, the Army sent him to Fort Hood where his unit deployed. I believe it was for fifteen months. During this deployment, while on a convoy, his vehicle rolled over an improvised explosive device (IED), and it detonated. Eventually, his unit returned home, and they began preparing for the next deployment, but due to the mission, his unit involuntarily extended him beyond his end date. Since he was not allowed to get out of the Army, and he had earned the rank of sergeant, he applied for Officer's Candidate School. The school accepted him, and he graduated earning the rank of second lieutenant. He was in his early forties, and with his background, I knew we were going to work hard.

CHAPTER 45

Balad, Iraq / Camp Anaconda

On September 3, 2009, Quanta gave birth to *Kyra Marie Hicks*. We were so happy that the hospital did not damage her arms, but unfortunately, after further examination, the doctor said that Kyra had a small hole in her heart. It would require surgery once she reached a certain age and weight. We were hurt but understood it could always be worse. I played with my pretty baby for three weeks, then it was time to leave.

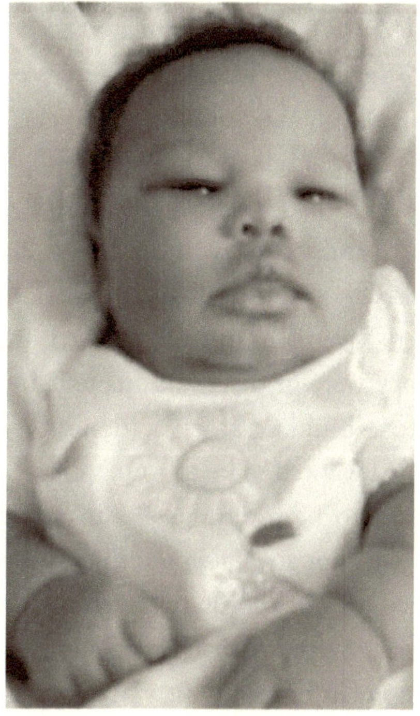

Kyra Marie Hicks

I met Lieutenant Baker at Fort Eustis and he drove us to Dulles International Airport. We flew eight hours to Frankfurt, Germany, then we sat there for two hours, before flying six more hours to Ali Al Salem, Kuwait. It was known as tent city, because this was where thousands of servicemembers and civilians connected with flights going stateside, Iraq, and other places. The compound was huge, and completely graveled with extra-large tents everywhere. Since the porta potties and showers were forty yards away from our tent, when I showered, I packed my toiletries in my rucksack (e.g., shower shoes). It was so hot, by the time I returned to my tent from the shower, I was sweating. The daytime temperature was over one hundred and twenty-five degrees. It cooled off at night to eight five degrees. Chow was available twenty-four hours a day, and it was good. Lieutenant Baker and I walked to the morale, welfare, and recreation center (MWR). I called home, watched a movie, ate popcorn, and enjoyed the air conditioning. There was also a Kentucky Fried Chicken, Pizza Hut, and Subway on the site.

On October 5, 2009, a bus drove us to the flight line to board a C130 military transport plane. The flight was full of personnel, and since it was night, the pilots flew without lights. It was an extremely uncomfortable forty-five-minute flight to Balad, Iraq (Camp Anaconda). A representative from our unit picked us up from the airport terminal. They were glad we had made it there safely. As the driver drove us to a building to sign for our rooms, Lieutenant Baker asked me, "If I wanted to be roommates?," and I replied, "No sir." I did not want to be roommates with anyone I worked for, plus I knew that with our strong work ethics, we would never stop working. We signed for our rooms and then the driver dropped me off first. My site was covered with graveled and filled with dozens of small trailers call combat housing units (CHUs). Closely surrounding the trailers were exceptionally large and tall slabs of something that resembled concrete. The porta potties and showers were at least forty yards away, so I showered and fell asleep. The next day, we met our company commander and first sergeant. They informed us that our soldiers worked in the emergency rooms of three hospitals where they processed casualty reports within those emergency rooms. After the meeting, Lieutenant Baker called our higher headquarters for guidance, but unfortunately, they did not know much about our mission either.

One of our hospitals was a mile walk down the road, so we put on our gear, grabbed our weapons, and walked down the street. I did not know what to expect, but to my surprise, the hospital was big and functioned similarly to a stateside hospital. We walked to the emergency room and met our soldiers. They were a five-person team which consisted of four males and one female from the Nashville, Tennessee National Guard. Lieutenant Baker and I learned that their main responsibility was to process casualty reports promptly and accurately. They introduced us to other hospital staff, and Lieutenant Baker and I walked back to our office.

CHAPTER 46

Mosul / Baghdad

Eager to learn our jobs, Lieutenant Baker suggested that we scheduled a flight to Mosul. I agreed, and later that day, a soldier drove us to the airport terminal. The terminal was closely surrounded by the same concrete structures as our living quarters. We scheduled a flight and I returned to my room to pack. A few hours later, we returned to the terminal because we had to check in two hours in advance. We sat down, watched television, and waited for an hour before our flight was ready. We then lined up for our mandatory briefing, before walking out the back door and entering one of the two medium sized passenger vans. The windows were tinted, and curtains hung from every window. I put in my ear plugs and rode four minutes to the flight line. When we arrived on the flightline, I walked off the van and boarded a large C5 military transport plane. It was another night flight, and we sat on the plane for thirty minutes before leaving. I did not know why, but once we departed it was a forty-five-minute flight to our second hospital. When we arrived a soldier that we knew met us at the airport terminal and it was nice to see her. She led us to the small one story building they called a hospital, where Lieutenant Baker and I met the rest of our soldiers.

They were a team of five female soldiers from our unit at Fort Eustis that we had helped prepare for this deployment. We talked about their mission, and afterwards, Lieutenant Baker and I walked to our trailers, and I fell asleep.

The next morning, we continued to observe how they functioned. As severely injured soldiers unexpectedly entered the emergency room, our soldiers assisted them. Outside of the hospital's front door and to the right was the chaplain's office, and twenty yards in front of those buildings were three tall slabs of concrete. The hospital and chaplain's office sat at the bottom of a valley. I thought the enemy had an excellent viewpoint of us and I was right; because right before any of us arrived, a mortar round hit the chaplain's office and a soldier was killed. Someone had painted a memorial on the slabs in honor of the soldier.

The entire area was undeveloped. We walked on gravel and the vehicles drove over unpaved roads. The dining facility was nice, but the walk there and back was a mile and a half. We spent three days training there before returning to Camp Anaconda. Days later, we flew to Camp Striker in Baghdad, which was the location of our third hospital. A young Air Force airmen picked us up from the terminal and we rode to their site. They were a five-person Air Force team from the 732 Casualty Liaison Team. I believe there were three females and two males. They were all active duty, and I do not remember where they were from. Their makeshift hospital was in the middle of nowhere. Concealed by camouflage nets and concrete slabs, they worked out of medium tents and one double wide trailer.

They were knowledgeable and thoroughly explained how they ran their operation. That evening, an airmen drove us to our sleep site. It was next to the airport terminal. We slept on a cot inside a large metal building resembling a warehouse. It was large enough to hold sixty people or more, and our filthy shower area and porta potties were twenty yards away from the warehouse. The next day, we walked one mile to their work site and continued training. When I was hungry, I settled for junk food; because I did not want to walk to their dining facility which was a mile away. After three days, we returned to home base and formulated a plan.

CHAPTER 47

What Was That

Our soldier's main responsibility was to process casualty reports accurately and promptly. Then they sent them to us for review and after we reviewed them, we would forward the reports to Kuwait. To further illustrate this process, in the movies when servicemembers died in combat, a military representatives drove to their homes and notified their next of kin. That process began with us initiating those reports. Lieutenant Baker and I typed a detailed policy outlining our duties and responsibilities. Then we gave a copy to each team, and they created a local policy mirroring our guidance.

We also began flying more. Since our soldiers often needed supplies, we traveled with a tough box. After sometimes sitting in the airport terminal for over an hour, the staff would announce that our flights were cancelled. If we were fortunate enough to board, we would sit on the plane for thirty minutes or longer due to potential enemy threat, bad weather or a bird problem. But more likely than not, we would have to exit the plane because the flight crew felt the plane was not safe to fly. One night we flew to Mosul, and I sat beside a chaplain. About twenty-five minutes into our flight, there was a loud noise, and a bright orange flame lit the sky. From the light's reflection, I saw the chaplain's face, and I could see that I was not the only person scared. I thought a rocket had hit our plane, but I was wrong. When we landed, the flight crew told us that there was a major mechanical issue. When I walked off the plane, I noticed that we had returned to our home base.

A soldier picked us up and drove us back to our rooms. I was glad to be back in my room. Unfortunately, the mattress on my twin sized bed was very worn. Every morning when I woke and stood up, my entire lower body ached for ten minutes. I had an infantry soldier as a roommate. He was also a staff sergeant that patrolled the outside of our gates. When I did see him in our room, we spoke but rarely held a conversation. He always looked stressed and angered. While at Camp Anaconda, whenever I walked anywhere, I knew exactly where the bunkers were in case of a rocket attack. To help with those types of attacks, the Army used a counter rocket, artillery, and mortar or a C-RAM. It resembled a tall metal tower with a very sophisticated weapons system attached to it. It had the ability to sense, warn, respond, and intercept incoming rounds. Even from afar, the warning sounds and how it intercepted incoming rounds were loud. If I ate at a certain dining facility, I had to walk past a C-RAM. It just so happened that one day as I was walking to a dining facility, the C-RAM intercepted some incoming rounds, and it sounded like very loud rapid gun fire. So, I dove to the ground and my face landed on my weapon. Seconds later, I looked up and noticed that the other soldiers never fell to the ground or ran to a bunker. I stood up, brushed myself off, and continued walking to the dining facility. As I walked, I wondered if I was being overly dramatic or if they were just being complacent.

CHAPTER 48

Twenty-Four Seven

On January 1, 2010, I earned the rank of sergeant first class. I was happy because this was a personal goal of mine. I celebrated and continued to focus on our mission. At the office, we began to notice that our soldiers and Air Force personnel were frequently calling with similar concerns. It was as if while I was assisting the team in Mosul with a question or concern, Lieutenant Baker was answering the same question for Camp Striker in Baghdad. This led to Lieutenant Baker and I creating an online battle box, which allowed us to communicate simultaneously and resolve problems more efficiently. When Lieutenant Baker and I worked out of our office, we walked three quarters of a mile one way to chow at least once a day. Our dining facilities were nice and huge, and before walking inside, I cleared my weapon to ensure there were no rounds in the chamber. Then we slung our weapons over our backs and walked inside. As we ordered food, I hated it when soldiers bent over, and their weapons barrel pointed at me. This would also happen when we sat down to eat, so I began asking for to go boxes and ate in my room.

Lieutenant Baker and I worked around the clock. One day, we were in the office when Lieutenant Baker received word that we could fly out to Baghdad in a Blackhawk helicopter. He was overly excited and asked if I wanted to go. I looked at him like he was crazy and said, "No sir!" We already had a flight scheduled and I did not see the rush. Except for another lieutenant and a sergeant, no one travelled as much as Lieutenant Baker and I. In addition, if there was a suspense on anything, we never missed it. It also helped that the administrative office responsible for processing our transactions worked in the same building as we did. Unfortunately, their office was disorganized and regularly lost time sensitive documents such as awards and evaluations. I always had to turn documents in twice. Our company commander and first sergeant knew of this but never done anything about it. One day, our brigade commander sent out an email, stating that if a unit submitted certain types of awards for processing (e.g., Purple Heart, Legion of Merit, Bronze Star), they must meet a certain level of responsibility. Lieutenant Baker and I both knew less than halfway into our tour we were going to meet that level of responsibility. We did not wait for our command to make this recommendation for us. That same day, Lieutenant Baker and I began drafting our own Bronze Star awards. Three days later, we gave them to our administrative office for review. Once our leadership read them, the leaders asked me to help them, and I did. After I finished, I told them that I had tried but they needed to do more to warrant such an award; because their level of responsibility did not meet the expectations, they dismissed the thought.

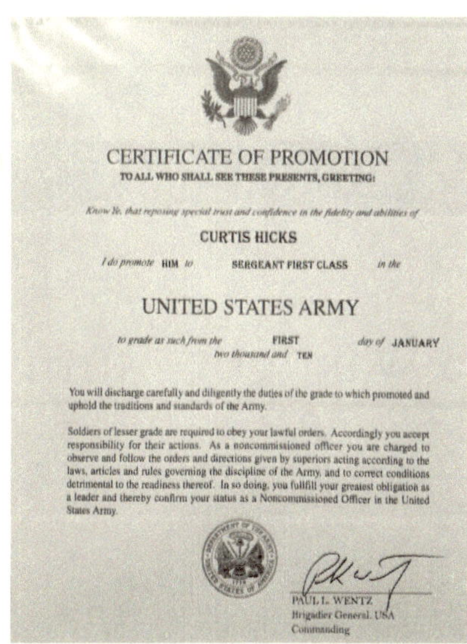

CHAPTER 49

It Was Not Funny

During my fifth month of this deployment, the unit granted me two weeks of leave, and I needed a break. Quanta picked me up from the airport and it felt great to be home. Jaylin was now in the second grade and Kyra was seven months old, and they both had really grown since the last time I'd seen them. The next morning, Jaylin had school and Quanta had a hair appointment, so I watched Kyra. Once Kyra realized her mom and sister were not home, she cried. I tried to play with her and hold her, but it did not work. She did not remember me and cried for forty-five minutes. It got so bad that I had to take her to Quanta. My two weeks flew by, and I returned to Iraq. A week later, Lieutenant Baker flew back to the states, and this was when I began to fly alone. One morning I flew to Mosul on a flight that had less than ten people onboard. It was a clear blue sky and I never liked days like this because we were highly visible. Near the flight crew sat a civilian lady, who had begun to conversate with them. She enjoyed their conversation so much that she stood up and walked into the cockpit area. Suddenly, and for no reason, the pilot began to drop our elevation and made hard turns left and right.

They all laughed and seemed to be having fun; however, I felt like they were playing with our lives, and it was unnecessary.

Thankfully, we arrived safely to Mosul, and I walked to the hospital. When I walked into the emergency room, I noticed a young soldier reading a textbook and completing what looked like schoolwork. Later that day, I talked to her and found out that she was enrolled in college, and she convinced me that I could do the same. A few days later when I returned to Camp Anaconda, I drove to our education center, and met with a counselor to see if I was eligible to enroll into Columbia Southern University. I was told that I would have to complete two different math classes as part of my enrollment. Fortunately for me these two classes were offered next door to our education center, and after completing both courses, I was able to successfully pass both exams.

Shortly after this, I was in my room sleeping when someone knocked on my door. It was an explosive ordnance disposal sergeant, who told me that a mortar round had landed between my combat housing unit and our showers, and they were there to prepare to blow it up. Twenty minutes later, there was a very loud explosion that shook the compound. From that point on, every time I walked to our showers, I wondered if a mortar round was heading my way.

CHAPTER 50

Come on Man

When Lieutenant Baker returned to Iraq, I was in Baghdad; however, we did speak over the phone, and he informed me that he was heading to Mosul. A couple of days later, when we were both back at Camp Anaconda. Lieutenant Baker told me that he had met with our company commander, and she told him there were two other hospitals in Iraq. The casualty team that managed those hospitals had redeployed and no one had been sent to replace them. Lieutenant Baker then proceeded to tell me that, "We were going to fill in at these two hospitals." I quickly replied with, "Sir this is too much. I ain't with all that work!" He looked at me and said, "Oh yes, you are Sergeant."I then said, "Hooah, Sir." I turned and walked into our building and sat at my desk in thought; because I now understood that this meant that we would be managing every hospital emergency room in Iraq. It also meant that we had more responsibility and would be traveling even more.

This brought me back to a few weeks prior, when I was walking through our building, and I saw my company commander. She told me that our administrative office had lost our awards, and due to time constraints, she needed me to retype the awards for Meritorious

Service Medals (MSM) instead of the Bronze Star Medals. I told her that I would not downgrade our awards, but I would retype them and resubmit them again. I believed this was unacceptable and I knew that her or the first sergeant's Bronze Star awards had not been lost.

As I continued to sit quietly in thought, I had a strange feeling that he had volunteered us to take over those two hospitals, and with this revelation, I became so mad that I lost focus. So, I told Lieutenant Baker that I was going to speak with our chaplain, and I did. I shared all my concerns with him, and he informed our battalion chain of command. From that point on my relationship with the company commander, first sergeant, and Lieutenant Baker changed, but I didn't care. My company commander, first sergeant, and their administrative office had only sixty days left in the country.

Lieutenant Baker and I flew to Baghdad to introduce ourselves to our new soldiers. They were a five-man team of active-duty soldiers from Fort Bragg, North Carolina. Their hospital was huge, and they knew their jobs very well. After our meeting, we flew from Baghdad to Talil, to meet another group of young soldiers from Fort Eustis. Although these soldiers had come from Fort Eustis like us, we did not know them. However, we understood that they needed help, and we were there to assist them. Their emergency room had a couple of severely injured soldiers, and it was not looking good, but after three days of training and closely monitoring the wellbeing of my soldiers, I was able to return to home base. I was glad to be back in my room again.

CHAPTER 51

I Would Not Have Guessed It

One night as I laid half asleep in bed, with my television on the Pentagon Channel, there was a special report that aired. The newscaster reported that a soldier had been killed by an IED in Afghanistan, but when he said the name of the soldier, I sat up and paid closer attention to what he was saying. The soldier's last night was unique and when they showed his face, I could not believe it. He was a soldier that I had put in the Army. So, I reached out to the Charlottesville Recruiting Station, and they confirmed that it was in fact him. I felt like sh$$!

I had met this soldier while he was in college. He had wanted to do something different and was interested in the medical field. He had told me quite often that, "He did not want to die in combat." and I understood. We had bonded for over eighteen months before he joined, and after he joined, we stayed in contact via email. He had met his wife in the Army and was happily married. The Charlottesville Recruiting Station sent me his picture and I still have it and our emails to this day.

Eight months into my tour, my company commander, first sergeant and their administrative office all redeployed, and were replaced by another unit. I was excited for the change; however, a month after their departure, I was sitting at my desk, when I received an email from Cameron or Kendrick asking me to call them as soon as possible. When I called, I was told that one of my best friends had died. He was also an active-duty sergeant first class that had been stationed in Germany. We had all grew up in JDUB together, and he had joined the Army two years before I did. Since, I worked in casualties, I reached out to the casualty office in Kuwait for help. They sent me his casualty report and it was still hard to believe. I told Lieutenant Baker what happened and explained that he was one of my best friends, but when I asked him if I could go to his funeral, his response was "I though you said Cameron was your best friend." Earlier in our tour, I had said that, and since I had said that he did not believe me. So, I walked into my new first sergeant's office and told him what happened. He apologized for my loss, and once he verified my story, he told me that, "I could go to his funeral." He also suggested that since there was a possibility that Lieutenant Baker and I could redeploy sooner than expected, that we brief our brigade commander on casualty operations, and after the briefing, I could leave Iraq and go to his funeral. I agreed. Afterwards, I believe our company commander informed Lieutenant Baker of our agreement.

The brigade was two levels above us, and a lieutenant and a platoon sergeant that worked at the company level had no business briefing a full bird colonel. However, our leadership knew that we understood casualty operations better than anyone else. At our meeting, the brigade commander told us that we completed tasks that were meant for our higher headquarters. He thanked us for a thorough briefing before Lieutenant Baker and I walked back to our office. When I walked into our building, I placed my vest and weapon in our office, and walked down the hallway into the first sergeant's office. I debriefed him on our meeting with the brigade commander, making sure to tell him how much the brigade commander appreciated the meeting and how well everything went. My first sergeant thanked me, told me to pack all my belongings, and I returned home for the funeral at the end of August 2010. After the funeral, I did not have to return to Iraq, and I was thankful for my first sergeant and his help.

Even though I returned home for the funeral of a close friend, it was good being home with my family. This time Kyra remembered me. My unit at Fort Eustis presented me with the Bronze Star Award and gave me some time off. I appreciated it and used the time off to schedule several doctor appointments. I had a complaint about my right arm, and after having a magnetic resonance image (MRI), the doctor found a tear and recommended surgery. In addition to having surgery, I was also diagnosed with post-traumatic stress disorder (PTSD). A few weeks later, I spoke to my career manager, and he sent me back to Fort Jackson, South Carolina.

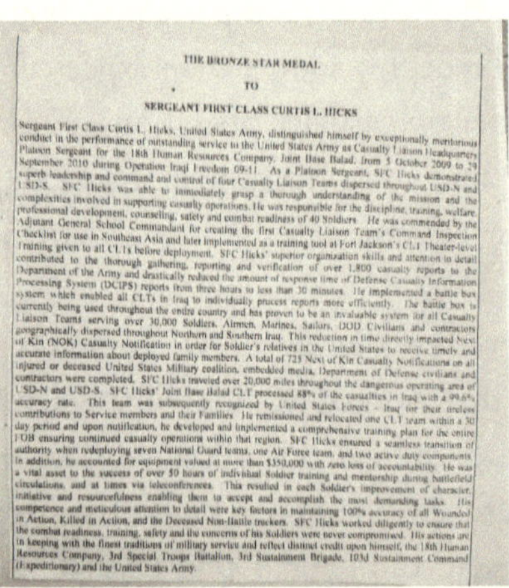

THE BRONZE STAR MEDAL

TO

SERGEANT FIRST CLASS CURTIS L. HICKS

Sergeant First Class Curtis L. Hicks, United States Army, distinguished himself by exceptionally meritorious conduct in the performance of outstanding service to the United States Army as Casualty Liaison Headquarters Platoon Sergeant for the 18th Human Resources Company, Joint Base Balad, from 5 October 2009 to 29 September 2010 during Operation Iraqi Freedom 09-11. As a Platoon Sergeant, SFC Hicks demonstrated superb leadership and command and control of four Casualty Liaison Teams dispersed throughout USD-N and USD-S. SFC Hicks was able to immediately grasp a thorough understanding of the mission and the complexities involved in supporting casualty operations. He was responsible for the discipline, training, welfare, professional development, counseling, safety and combat readiness of 40 Soldiers. He was commended by the Adjutant General School Commandant for creating the first Casualty Liaison Team's Command Inspection Checklist for use in Southeast Asia and later implemented as a training tool at Fort Jackson's CLT Theater-level Training given to all CLTs before deployment. SFC Hicks' superior organization skills and attention to detail contributed to the thorough gathering, reporting and verification of over 1,800 casualty reports to the Department of the Army and drastically reduced the amount of response time of Defense Casualty Information Processing System (DCIPS) reports from three hours to less than 30 minutes. He implemented a battle box system which enabled all CLTs in Iraq to individually process reports more efficiently. The battle box is currently being used throughout the entire country and has proven to be an invaluable system for all Casualty Liaison Teams serving over 30,000 Soldiers, Airmen, Marines, Sailors, DOD Civilians and contractors geographically dispersed throughout Northern and Southern Iraq. This reduction in time directly impacted Next of Kin (NOK) Casualty Notification in order for Soldier's relatives in the United States to receive timely and accurate information about deployed family members. A total of 725 Next of Kin Casualty Notifications on all injured or deceased United States Military coalition, embedded media, Department of Defense civilians and contractors were completed. SFC Hicks traveled over 20,000 miles throughout the dangerous operating area of USD-N and USD-S. SFC Hicks' Joint Base Balad CLT processed 88% of the casualties in Iraq with a 99.6% accuracy rate. This team was subsequently recognized by United States Forces – Iraq for their tireless contributions to Service members and their Families. He remissioned and relocated one CLT team within a 30 day period and upon notification, he developed and implemented a comprehensive training plan for the entire FOB ensuring continued casualty operations within that region. SFC Hicks ensured a seamless transition of authority when redeploying seven National Guard teams, one Air Force team, and two active duty components. In addition, he accounted for equipment valued at more than $350,000 with zero loss of accountability. He was a vital asset to the success of over 50 hours of individual Soldier training and mentorship during battlefield circulations, and at times via teleconferences. This resulted in each Soldier's improvement of character, initiative and resourcefulness enabling them to accept and accomplish the most demanding tasks. His competence and meticulous attention to detail were key factors in maintaining 100% accuracy of all Wounded in Action, Killed in Action, and the Deceased Non-Battle trackers. SFC Hicks worked diligently to ensure that the combat readiness, training, safety and the concerns of his Soldiers were never compromised. His actions are in keeping with the finest traditions of military service and reflect distinct credit upon himself, the 18th Human Resources Company, 3rd Special Troops Battalion, 3rd Sustainment Brigade, 103d Sustainment Command (Expeditionary) and the United States Army.

Bronze Star Write-Up

Bronze Star Medal

CHAPTER 52

369th Adjutant General Battalion, Fort Jackson, South Carolina

In December of 2010, we moved back to Fort Jackson, South Carolina and after finding a place to live, I began working for the 369th Adjutant General Battalion. I in processed and met with my battalion command sergeant major, who informed me that I was there to perform duties as an instructor. However, he needed an office manager and asked me about my background. So, I showed him my evaluations where I had served in this capacity numerous times, and after our meeting, he appointed me as his senior human resources manager.

I worked for Mr. Griffin who was a retired Army veteran, and from my first impression, he seemed like a cool guy. I also managed three sergeants that were also cool. Our main concerns were outdated policy letters and improper slotting of our personnel. We manage to correct and update our policies and the office began to function well. Since our workload was light, I had surgery on my right arm, which limited my ability to do physical training. So, I continued working towards completing my bachelor's degree. I also helped and encouraged my sergeants to do the same.

CHAPTER 53

Barbershop Talk

One day while I was at work, I saw a sergeant who had a nice haircut. So, I asked him, "Who cut his hair?" He told me the name of the barbershop and his barber's name. A few days later, I drove to the shop, which was a ten-minute drive from Fort Jackson. When I arrived, I walked in and introduced myself to the barber I was there to see. As I waited, I heard him, and others speaking in Arabic. I learned that they were Muslims, and he began to cut my hair regularly. I looked forward to returning to the barbershop; because I really enjoyed the conversations that were had in the barbershop, especially the ones they had about Islam. When my barber spoke about Islam, people listened, and I began to do the same. Afterwards, I began asking questions and researching what he discussed. My barber also gave me books to read and cassette disks to listen to. This continued for well over a year, and in December of 2012, I visited a local Mosque, met with an imaum, took my shahada, and became a Muslim. I immediately began to learn from my Muslim brothers, and it felt empowering. I read the Quran, Bible, and bought books, and cassette disks related to: Black history, politics, racism, health, American history, American law, and much more.

I studied something meaningful every day and shared it with my family. One example being that Jaylin did not like her hair permed, because it burnt her hair and scalp. I learned that the perm was very unhealthy for her hair and recommended that she go natural. Jaylin did her own research and agreed. We knew the transition would be challenging, because she could not fully extend her right arm to reach the top of her head. So, I told her that I would help her and when she needed her hair twisted, she told me what to do and I done it. Additionally, I learned that Black children spent less time studying than other children by a wide margin. Therefore, during the summer of Jaylin's seventh grade year, she spent more than half of her time learning. She also read books and she had a college student who tutored her in math. Since Jaylin was planning to go to college, that summer, she also agreed to take the practice SAT.

CHAPTER 54

Jaylin and Kyra

That summer Jaylin and I drove to Florida. We met my friend Kendrick at Disney World again. But this time around, Kendrick and Jaylin convinced me to ride a rollercoaster. This was not something that I want to do, but I done it for Jaylin. When it was our turn to board the rollercoaster ride, we sat down and buckled our seatbelts, and slowly rolled off at an incline. But as we crept closer to the top, I looked around and said, "Oh sh$$!," just as we hit full speed. I hollered and cursed the entire time, while they laughed at me. When I got off the ride, my legs were shaking, and I noticed that my baby was laughing so hard that it brought her to tears. We all had fun that day and these are memories that I will cherish and never forget.

Upon our return, Kyra was old enough and weight enough for us to schedule a date to have her surgery. As the time for her surgery became closer, we all felt horrible that our baby would have to be cut on. On the day of her surgery, we drove to Charleston, South Carolina, where Kyra's surgery would be done at The Medical University of South Carolina (MUSC). That day I remember Kyra being upbeat, and she did not show any signs of fear. On the other hand, Quanta and I were obviously overly concerned. Kyra spent three days in the hospital after her surgery. It was a difficult three days but thanks to Allah her surgery was a success.

CHAPTER 55

Human Resources Instructor

After two successful years as the office manager, it was time for me to become an instructor. However, before I could instruct, I had to complete a two-week course that taught me how to perform on the platform as an instructor. I successfully completed the course, and in January of 2012, I officially became an instructor. I would be teaching the same course that I had completed as a private. My mornings began at 0445 hours and my workday began at 0520 hours. After walking through the soldier's barracks, we all formed up outside, where other leaders and I marched our troops to a large grassy field and done physical fitness. Afterwards, the soldiers showered and ate chow before attending class.

Since class was already in session, I shadowed other instructors. I walked in and out of every classroom listening and learning. Until one day when a civilian instructor asked me, "If I wanted to teach one of her blocks of instruction?" I agreed and taught a portion of the class. Afterwards, she said that "I had done a great job and was one of the best she had heard." Not long after that, I began teaching every day. I had twenty-seven students in my classroom. Class began at 0830 hours and ended at 1600 hours. Soldiers paid attention and done well. After class, I met my soldiers at their barracks, and I taught them how to properly execute a military funeral. On the weekends, we would travel throughout South Carolina performing funeral details. After a long five weeks, the human resources course ended with a three-day field exercise.

When I served as the office manager, I enjoyed going to our soldier's graduation ceremonies. It was a chance to support the troops as well as get out of the office. Plus, I also enjoyed listening to the commencement speech. The speakers were usually instructors, but I believe that the civilian instructors and senior leadership also spoke occasionally. One day my first sergeant held a meeting at our soldier's barracks. I do not remember what it was about, but I do remember the two instructors that complained about always having to give commencement speeches. They reminded me of the sergeants I worked with when I was a recruiter. As this topic began to dominate the conversation, I sat there quietly and listened, because I knew the days of me volunteering to do anything were over. Plus, I made it known that I would be retiring very soon. A few moments later, with a grin, one of the staff sergeants that had been complaining, asked me, "If I wanted to do it?" Without giving it any thought, I said, "That I would do it." The other leaders in the room were surprised by my response, but I wasn't.

During the following weeks, Quanta and I worked on my speech. I felt it had to be authentic, not too long, practical, and inspiring. I finished my first draft and read it to Quanta as she video recorded me. Afterwards, we replaced hard to pronounce words, listened to my voice tone and checked my posture. After weeks of modifications and practice, we agreed that I had a quality speech. I did not let anyone else read it. On graduation day, I was a little nervous as soldiers, family members, instructors, and senior leadership filled the auditorium. The ceremony began and ten minutes later, the sergeant introduced me by reading my biography. Then he called me to the podium, and after my speech, I received a very loud round of applause. As I walked back to my seat on stage, I felt like it was a huge success. A few minutes later, the ceremony ended, and I walked off the stage and began to congratulate the soldiers. As I made my way through the crowd, the instructors told me that my speech was great. Mr. Griffin said it was excellent and it had him on the edge of his seat. He also said that "I set a new standard and that the others had to step it up." When I walked out of the auditorium, my school's sergeant major wanted to speak with me. She told me that, "That was one of the best commencement speeches she had ever heard." She then asked me, "If I wanted to speak at other ceremonies on the post?" I said, "Yes, Sergeant Major!" I also thanked her and felt honored that she had asked me to do so.

CHAPTER 56

Nineteenth Year in The Army

I continued instructing and graduated one more class. I had also reached my nineteenth year in the Army, and since I was retiring, the Army normally allowed soldiers twelve months to prepare. However, this was at the discretion of the commander. I forwarded my retirement paperwork to our administrative office and emailed my battalion command sergeant major to ask him when I could begin to prepare for retirement. He emailed me back and said, "Two weeks prior to my retirement date." I thought he was crazy, but when I spoke to my first sergeant and the school's sergeant major, they both echoed the same thing.

I drove home and made a couple of phone calls. I reached out to Sergeant First Class Warren for advice, and it helped. I also spoke to Command Sergeant Major Evans, who suggested that I speak with my battalion commander, and after multiple senior enlisted leaders said no, I had nothing to lose. So, I informed my chain of command that I planned to speak with our battalion commander, and it was not a problem. The day I walked into his office, we talked for over an hour. During this time, I told him that I had a wife and two children and that I needed time to find a job and complete my bachelor's degree before retiring. My battalion commander was married, and our children were of similar age, so he allowed me to begin preparing for retirement immediately. He granted me eleven months of terminal leave and told me to check in with him once a week. I said, "I will Sir" and I thanked him.

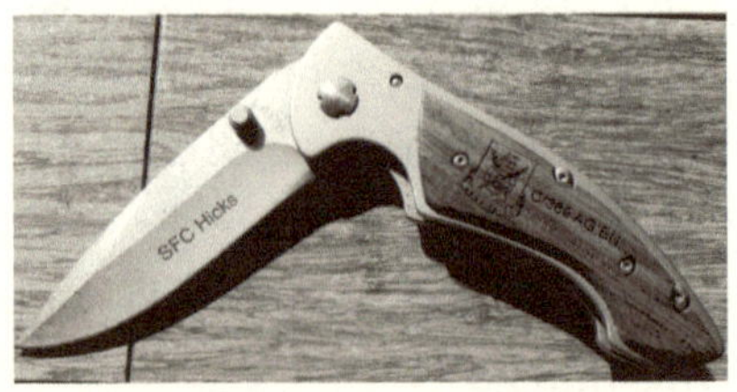

Sergeant First Class Hicks

I drove home and began applying for federal jobs. I also scheduled multiple doctor appointments and continued my education. In March of 2013, I earned my bachelor's degree in business administration from Columbia Southern University. While on terminal leave, I enrolled into a course at Midlands Technical College called The Society for Human Resource Management (SHRM). It was a five-month course that measured human resource knowledge. The knowledge they measured related to those that worked as a civilian human resources manager. Obtaining this certification meant I was a human resource's subject matter expert.

I had class one night a week. My classmates had been working as civilian human resources managers for over twenty years. Out of twenty plus students, there was only one other veteran in the class, and he was a retired Army officer.

In this course, I learned about unemployment, affirmative action, human services, the American Disability Act, payroll, human resource issues, employee insurance and a vast number of other subjects. Since all this information was foreign to me, I studied six to seven days a week for six to eight hours a day. When the course ended, I received a certificate of completion. Then, I selected a date, May 6, 2013, and scheduled my exam. On test day, I completed a three-hour long exam which consisted of one hundred and eighty-five multiple-choice questions. For each question, I had to select the best possible answers. It was incredibly challenging, and I fell short; however, I viewed it as a success; because I had never worked in any of those positions, and I scored well. After that, I enrolled into the University of Phoenix, for one night a week, and majored in Criminal Justice Administration.

Retirement Award

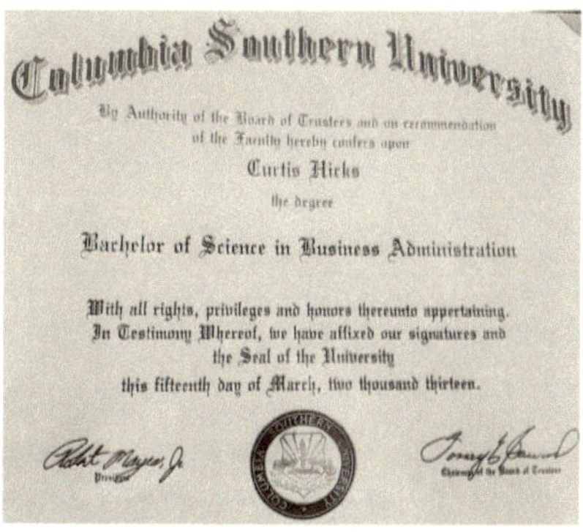

Bachelor in Business Administration

CHAPTER 57

South Carolina Department of Corrections

Once a week, I checked in with my battalion commander to let him know how I was doing, and in June of 2013, I began working at The Broad River Correctional Institution. It was a level three prison and I served as an administrative assistant for the warden, although I did have a supervisor, and she was sharp. She gave me a tour of the facility so that I would be familiar with the institution. The tour included a walk through the horticulture area, print shop, commissary, dining facility, and mailroom. My job was to process paperwork coming into our office from various departments, respond to an inmate's handwritten request about whatever it was they asked about, serve inmates court ordered documents to sign, pick up mail, type monthly awards for various departments, and set up and maintain a filing system.

In addition to these office duties, I was also responsible for processing correspondents regarding the misconduct of correctional officers and staff. When these incidents occurred, I would type an official document explaining what occurred and scheduled a date and time for the officer and any other person involved or acting as a witness to speak with the warden. I thought that it was cool that two of the tasks that I was assigned to do required me to use a typewriter. I quickly notice that each department had good staff members and that the chain of command was solid. In fact, it was evident that everyone understood the seriousness of their positions.

These traits were also emulated by the inmates that worked in the various areas throughout the facility. Inmates made license and name plates, grew vegetables and flowers, washed and waxed cars, cooked, and cut grass among various other jobs. I ordered a Washington Redskins' desk name plate and two personalized license plates. They done a good work.

My supervisor and I worked well together, and the paperwork was consistently being processed efficiently and was rarely misplaced. Staff members developed even more confidence in our office. By this time, I had been on the job for three months. A position at the institution became available, and my supervisor was interested. She applied, interviewed, and was hired. She was happy and I was happy for her. A month later, I interviewed for her position and the warden hired me. I was thankful that after three months he had enough trust in me to promote me to a supervisory position.

I can vividly recall on one day while I was at work, a Black correctional officer walked into our office. She spoke to me and said that she was there to meet with the warden. During our brief conversation, she said that "She wanted to meet me because the other staff members always talked about me in such a positive manner, that she thought I was White. I gave a slight grin and said, "No, I am Black."

On September 30, 2013, I officially retired from The United States Army, and I now only reported to the warden. The warden was not only fair, but he also solved problems, and security and safety were his top two priorities. We talked often, and he told me that his *daddy* was also a warden. In fact, he had grown up at the same institution that we worked at. Years ago, the institution had a house on the premises for the warden to live in, and some of the inmates helped raise him. He referred to them as house boys, who had helped him with his homework, cooked the best fried chicken, cleaned his house, and covered for him when he was in trouble.

CHAPTER 58

Inmates

The office was functioning well, and we eventually hired an assistant. I introduced her to everyone and began to thoroughly train her. She was nice, funny and she learned fast. Since her background was in corrections, she quickly grasped everything, but one day we were talking about being forgetful, and I said to her, "That while I was in the Army, we said that if you write everything down, you won't forget it." Normally, when I said that to people they agreed; however, she did not agree and said, "Not if I forget where I wrote it down!" I thought that was funny.

One of her duties was to check and pick up the mail which meant that she would have to walk on the yard. Although she was fully capable of protecting herself, I asked her to pick up the mail before 0900 hours. During this time there were little to no inmates around and I felt she would be safer. After lunch I would walk to the mailroom just to stretch my legs and because we often received documents that needed an inmate's signature. When the inmate being served was a part of the general population, we would both serve the inmate. Because some of the inmates were known for assaulting females, I did not let her serve paperwork to inmates housed in lockup. There was a procedure that we followed which required me to call lockup and schedule a date and time to serve the inmate. The personnel that worked in lockup would then schedule a time because the correctional officers had to prep the inmate. Thirty minutes prior to our scheduled meeting, I walked over to the lockup facility and put on my body gear and face protection. A few moments later, two correctional officers would slowly walk a shackled inmate down a long hallway and into an office. Both of the correctional officers would remain in the room. I would then introduce myself, give the inmate a copy of the document, explained why he needed to sign the document, and once the inmate signed the paperwork, my mission was complete. However, if the inmate did not want to sign the paperwork, I did not try to force him to. I would simply thank everyone for their time and returned back to my office.

Once a week I stood at our office door and watched the new inmates in process. I noticed that seven out of the ten new inmates were Black men of all ages. I also walked into our dining facility weekly. I knew the staff and wanted to say hello. I quickly learned that the inmates knew who I was, but I did not know them. When they called me, "Mr. Hicks," I spoke and continued walking. With so many inmates around, I felt defenseless and outnumbered, so I kept my head on a swivel. When I walked over to look at the food, I maintained my facial expression, but it always looked so nasty, and the tough looking guys serving food with sharp silverware did not help either. My stay was never long because I felt uncomfortable and I'm sure that it showed.

One day I was talking with a coworker, and when I turned to walk out of her office, I looked on top of a metal filing cabinet and saw a large dictionary. I walked over and opened it and noticed that it was published in 1953. One of my favorite movies was <u>Malcolm X</u>, and in the movie, there is a scene that showed an inmate encouraging another inmate to read the entire dictionary. The dictionary he told him to read was written around 1953. He also asked the inmate, "To look up the words black and white and how they were defined." In the movie, the dictionary viewed the color Black as impoverished and evil while white was innocent, pure, and clean. When I checked the definitions in the dictionary I held, it said the same. So, I cut the pages out, brought them home and talked to Jaylin about it.

The assaults on female staff members continued which concerned my assistant. I understood her concerns and when she told me that another position at the institution had become available, and that she had interviewed for it, I supported her decision. I also knew that with her quality skill set and pleasant personality that the other agency would be interested in hiring her. A week later, she told the warden that she was resigning. We were happy for her and wished her the best. I was not sure why, but after her departure, we did not hire another assistant. The workload and environment became too much to manage mentally and physically, and after a year and four months, I too was drained and had to resign in November of 2014.

|-mou*thz'|. *Slang.* A person who talks carelessly and at length.

black |blăk| *n.* **1. a.** The darkest or least bright of the series of colors that runs through all the shades of gray to white; the opposite of white; the darkest of all colors. **b.** Clothing of this color, especially for mourning: *a man dressed in black.* **2.** Any member of a Negroid people; a Negro. —*adj.* **black·er, black·est. 1.** Of or nearly of the color black. **2.** Without light: *a black, moonless night.* **3.** Belonging to an ethnic group having dark skin, especially Negroid. **4.** Gloomy; depressing: *a black day; black thoughts.* **5.** Often **Black.** Marked by disaster: *The stock market crashed on Black Friday.* **6.** Deserving of or indicating censure or dishonor: *the industry's blackest record as a polluter of the rivers.* **7.** Evil; wicked: *black deeds.* **8.** Angry; sullen: *a black look on his face.* **9.** Served without cream or the North Riding, NE York, England.

white (hwīt) *adj.* **whit·er, whit·est** **1** Having the color produced by reflection of all the rays of the solar spectrum, as from a finely powdered surface; having the color of new snow: opposed to *black.* **2** Light or comparatively light in color; specifically, light-colored as opposed to *red: white* wine. **3** Bloodless; ashen: *white* with rage. **4** Very fair; blond. **5** Silvery, hoary, or gray, as with age. **6** Covered with snow; snowy. **7** Made of silver; also unburnished, as silverwork. **8** Habited in white clothing: *white* nuns. **9** Not intentionally wicked or evil; not malicious or harmful: a *white* lie. **10** Figuratively, free from spot or stain; innocent: a *white* soul. **11** Incandescent; being at white heat. **12** Blank; unmarked by ink: said of a space in an advertisement or the like. **13** Having a light-colored skin; Caucasian: opposed especially to *Negro,* but often to the yellow, brown, or red races of men. **14** Of, pertaining to, or governed by the white race: *white* supremacy. **15** *Colloq.* Fair and honorable; straightforward; honest. **16** Propitious; auspicious: a rare meaning. **17** In certain European countries, constitutional; conservative, as a party; opposed to the radicals or revolutionaries. See synonyms under PALE². — *n.* **1** That color seen when sunlight is reflected without sensible absorption of any of the visible rays of the spectrum; the color in the scale of grays which is entirely without hue and is the opposite of *black.* **2** The state or condition of being white; whiteness; figuratively, innocence; truth. **3** The white or light-colored part of something; specifically, the albumen of an egg, or the white part of the eyeball. **4** Anything that is white or nearly white, as cloth or garments; in the plural, a white uniform or outfit: The sailor wore his summer *whites.* **5** White wine. **6** A white paint or pigment; hence, by comparison, a color approaching pure white in its effect. **7** In chess or checkers, the white or light men, or the player who has them. **8** *pl.* Flour made from the finest and whitest part of the wheat. **9** *pl. Printing* Blank spaces in a picture, plate, mold, etc. **10** In archery, the outermost ring of a target; also, a hit on that ring, scoring one point. **11** A member of a fair-skinned race; especially, one of the Caucasian race as distinguished from a Negro, an Indian, a Chinese, etc. **12** In some European countries, a member of a party opposed to the radicals or revolutionaries; a conservative. **13** *pl. Pathol.* Leukorrhea. — *v.t.* **whit·ed, whit·ing 1** To make white; whiten; bleach. **2** *Printing* To make or leave blank spaces in, as between lines or about an illustration: often with *out:* to *white* out a column. [OE *hwīt*]

White (hwīt) **Andrew** 1832–1918, U.S.

CHAPTER 59

Janice Loved Her Boys

I called my friend Mr. Griffin and we met at Fort Jackson for lunch. At the time, he was the commander at a local American Legion, and he was looking for a finance officer, so he asked me, "If I was interested?" Since I was not sure, he asked me "To drive pass the legion one day to check it out." I did and I had fun. I enjoyed the environment, and a few weeks later I decided to join their American Legion. After becoming a member in February of 2015, the members voted me in as their new finance officer.

In March of 2015, I drove to Portsmouth to visit my friends, before driving to Conway to visit my Aunt Mary. When I drove into her yard, I noticed that her trailer was different, it was newer; however, when I looked at the shed, it looked the same. I knocked on her back door and when Aunt Mary opened it, I said, "Hey Aunt Mary it's Curtis, Janice's son, do you remember me?" She smiled and she did remember me, although it had been over twenty years since I had last seen her. We exchanged pleasantries and were happy to see each other. As I entered and sat down, I could tell that Aunt Mary's style of living was still the same, simple! She had one small television that we did not turn on, and I was sure that she did not have cable;

however, she seemed very content and looked well. She was ninety-five years old, lived alone and moved around without the use of a cane. She asked me about Jason, and I told her he was doing fine. As we reminisced, I notice Aunt Mary's memory was still intact. She talked about events that had happened over thirty years ago, some of them I had forgotten about but when she mentioned them, I was able to remember them as she spoke. She also talked about how evil Augustine was and how Janice loved her boys. I asked her what her keys were to living a life of longevity. She told me to "Cook my own food and not to drink soft drinks." We talked a little longer and then I drove back to Portsmouth.

CHAPTER 60

South University School of Pharmacy

I returned back to South Carolina and continued my volunteer work. In December of 2015, I received a phone call about a position I had applied for at the South University School of Pharmacy. On the day of my interview, I walked to the school's admissions office and introduced myself. A lady then walked me to a conference room, and I sat down. A video teleconference was also set up for two staff members from their Savannah, Georgia campus to take part in the interview. During my interview, every staff member and doctor that worked there was in the conference room, which was a total of nine people. The dean of the school led the interview, and as I answered their questions, I noticed that the Black doctors were more interested in me than the others. After my interview, I did not expect to hear from anyone regarding the job; because I felt that the doctor that they said I would be working for was not interested in me. Surprisingly, someone from their Savannah campus called and offered me the position and I accepted the job as their clinical coordinator.

My supervisor paired me with my counterpart in Savannah and he trained me on what would be expected of me and my job responsibilities. My job required me to complete the student's class schedules, however, this was not as easy as it sounded. The South University School of Pharmacy offered a three-year program and during the first two years of the program the students completed courses on campus. There was never an issue with scheduling students for courses on campus, but when it was time for students to complete their internships during their third year, they made unique requests. The second phase of my job was also to set up new hospital contracts allowing students to complete internships all over the United States, which could become difficult when trying to meet every student's request. After completing their internship portion of the program, the students would graduate and earn their Doctorate in Pharmacy degree.

I enjoyed the students, and while most were from South Carolina and Georgia, others were from New York, Michigan, South Korea, and Africa. I worked with nine doctors and three of them were Black. I did not have a problem with anyone, and I showed the same respect to everyone; however, I knew half of the White doctors felt uneasy around me. My favorite doctor was a Black man from Washington D.C. I told him I was from Portsmouth. He was the one that kept everyone sane, and the students loved him. He helped everyone that walked into his office. We became good friends, and I began to ask him for advice as well.

One day, I was talking to my supervisor about volunteering. He told me that he viewed volunteering as a waste of time. In comparison, when I talked to my favorite doctor about our American Legion, he thought it was great and wanted to visit. One day after work, he asked me "If I wanted to drive to the legion for a beer?" I agreed and we sat at the bar with four other veterans and had a great time. After that, the veterans at the American Legion nicknamed me "Doc" or "Professor."

One Saturday, I had to work, and my favorite doctor was preparing to give a presentation on marijuana. As students and staff members sat in the auditorium, he walked in, turned on a song by Rick James titled, _Mary Jane_ and slowly walked down the steps and up to the podium. I thought it was smooth, and during his lecture, I sat beside the doctor I worked for who leaned over to me and said that "He did not support legalizing marijuana unless he could make money." I nodded north and south, but I did not comment. I was not sure why, but he then switched the conversation to drug trafficking. He laughed and said, "If anyone drove through Georgia with New York tags, the police would pull them." Again, I listened and did not respond. I did not ask him how he knew that, but after my experiences in Georgia, that did not surprise me.

CHAPTER 61

My Family

In March of 2016, I received a phone call from Jason telling me that our Aunt Mary had passed away. She was ninety-eight years old and the last of my mother's siblings. I felt bad and wished that I had spent more time with her. For personal reasons, I was unable to attend her funeral. However, Jason and his family went, and after the funeral, Jason called me, and we talked about the funeral. He also told me that Augustine was there. After our conversation, I hung up the phone and thought about Aunt Mary.

Three months after Aunt Mary's passing, my family held their annual family reunion in Conway, North Carolina. I called Jason and asked if he was going. Unfortunately, he had other plans and was not able to make it. So, my family and I drove up to where my family had reserved a building to meet everyone. When I walked inside, there were people cooking in the kitchen. One of them was Patricia, who was a friend of our family. Because she was busy, we spoke, and she continued working. It was good to see everyone, since it had been over twenty-five years since I last seen them. I sat down next to Quanta and next my cousin Sweet Potato, and after speaking to her, I played a couple of games before sitting back down. When I looked around, I noticed that my family members were barely interacting with each other. It appeared that everyone that lived in Portsmouth sat together, and the same thing was happening with those that lived in Washington D.C., Hampton, Virginia, and Conway. The atmosphere felt very uneasy.

As I walked around, I realized that for it to have supposed to be a day of fun and laughter, Patricia kept a frown on her face. I sat back down but I became tired of sitting, so, I walked outside to my truck, stood there, and began talking to another one of my cousins. As we talked, she looked at me and said, "Curtis you do know that Patricia is living on land that belongs to you and Jason?" She also informed me that Jason has known about this since my Aunt Mary's funeral. I told her that Jason and I had talked on the day of Aunt Mary's funeral, but we did not talk about this.

We walked back into the building, sat down and about thirty minutes later, someone suggested driving to our loved one's grave sites, so we did. It was a five-minute drive to the cemetery and as we continued to reminisce, I notice that only my family from Portsmouth drove to the grave site. Afterwards, my cousin and I drove another five minutes to Aunt Mary's trailer. While we were standing outside, she asked me if "I remembered the shed?," and I said, "Yes." I also told her that I had visited Aunt Mary in March of 2015. A few moments later Patricia arrived, continuing to look mad, and walked inside Aunt Mary's trailer. My cousin and I continued to stand outside talking, before we left. I thanked my cousin and my family and drove to my mother in laws house. I thought that it was very odd that Patricia and I never engaged in conversation that day.

That same evening, I called Jason and told him what our cousin had told me. He said he was aware and thought that he had told me. I asked him to meet me later that night in Portsmouth, and so that we could visit with another one of our cousins. When we arrived, she told us that "After Aunt Mary's death, the family tried to reach us, but we could not be found, and since we could not be found, the family decided to give Aunt Mary's trailer, land, money, and personal belongings to Patricia." My cousin also said that "Aunt Mary had money stashed away in her trailer and in the bank totaling thousands of dollars, the names of the adults that used the money for themselves, and that her grandchildren never received a dime." We thanked her and I drove back to my mother in law's house. The next day, Quanta and I drove back to South Carolina.

When we returned home, I called Jason and told him that the following weekend I wanted to drive back to Conway to talk to Patricia. He said, "Cool!" So, on Saturday morning I drove to Portsmouth. That afternoon, Jason and I drove to Conway. When I knocked on the back door, Patricia opened it, but when she saw our faces, she had a look of concern on her face. We spoke and hugged, before walking inside the trailer where Patricia, Jason and I sat down, and we all talked. I do not know why but Patricia asked us if "We remembered her being a drunk?" I said, "No," but I did and wondered why she asked that of all things. Patricia also talked about Augustine and asked how we felt about her. What she did not know was that I viewed them both the same and that was as opportunists.

I began asking questions about Aunt Mary, and the more I asked, the more Patricia's tone changed. With an attitude she said, "Aunt Mary was the only momma I knew." Jason and I did not comment and began talking about something else. Jason and I knew Aunt Mary did not have any children. A few minutes later, Patricia's daughter came over, and we all continued to talk. On the wall hung a picture of Aunt Mary. Patricia asked me if I wanted it, and I said yes. Before I walked out the door, I hugged Patricia's daughter, but as I looked into her eyes, she was looking at her mother with concern. Jason and I walked out the door and drove back to Portsmouth.

On that Sunday morning, I drove back to South Carolina, and after talking to Jason, I wanted to speak with a probate attorney. So,

I met with a probate attorney in South Carolina, but they did not cover North Carolina; therefore, I emailed and called Murfreesboro and Conway probate attorneys, courts, local churches, and the nursing home Aunt Mary lived in, and explained to them what had happened. The courthouse was helpful; however, the probate attorneys told me that I had a fight on my hands, and the local churches did not want to go anywhere near this.

CHAPTER 62

Let's Make a Deal

At work I tried to focus my thoughts on my job, and I had to. At the time we had quality internships in place for students to complete. Our most prized being the Veterans Affairs Hospitals, and while the experience was unique, there were never enough openings for more of our students to take part in. Instead, only a select few were offered this experience, and although I do not remember how he made his determination, my supervisor selected which students would go. One day, I suggested to my supervisor that we consider establishing a contract with Kirkland Correctional Facility. It was a level three prison and twenty-five minutes away from the school. I also explained to him that when I worked in corrections, medical personnel always done more with less, and that they could use the assistance from our students. I strongly believed that this would provide another quality and unique experience, but my supervisor's facial expression told me that he was hesitant. So, I reached out to the Kirkland's medical staff, explained what we had in mind, and scheduled a meeting over the phone. The meeting was a success and it led to us visiting the prison. On that day, we met the medical staff and saw exactly where our students would work. We were assured that they would not be in harm's way and would never be in direct contact with an inmate. Afterwards, my supervisor finally got on board with it. After going back and forth with modifications, I finally set up a written agreement between both agencies, and sixty days later, Kirkland began to instruct our students.

Quarterly, I travelled out of state for conferences where we discussed various concerns and ate well. However, because of my background and me being new to the medical field, I often had little input. In addition to attending conferences, we held them at our school and doctors from the surrounding areas attended. We also hosted job fairs which were helpful to our students, although eighty percent of our student's already had a job lined up for them before they graduated. This was also a great time for me personally and professionally, because on May 31, 2016, I earned my bachelor's degree in criminal justice administration from Phoenix University.

By now, I was very proficient at my job, and our students appreciated my efforts. In fact, they often bought me gifts to show their appreciation. During spring break, one student had flown back to Africa to visit his family. He brought me back a beautiful artifact. I thanked him and I was very appreciative. As time progressed, I became good friends with six to eight minority students, who had all spoke about previous challenges with class schedules and racism.

**Bachelors in Criminal Justice
Administration**

CHAPTER 63

That Tasted Good

Unexpectedly and with deep regret, my favorite doctor passed away. I felt sorry for his family, the staff members, and our students. During the same week of his death, our work atmosphere quickly changed for the worst. It led to multiple doctors and administrators resigning and leaving for other positions. As I tried to focus on the job instead of the people I worked with, it became more difficult by the day. Then one day, I met Dr. Anand who was a new hire. I immediately noticed that his demeanor was calm and quite easy going. I introduced myself and we immediately connected. He had grown up overseas and had lived in the United States for the past fifteen or so years. We began to talk every day and learned that we both had families and a strong passion for health. We talked about health more than anything else. He told me that he began his day by taking multivitamins and drinking herbal drinks, and Sundays, he gave his digestive system a break by not eating food at all.

One weekend, our employer paid for all the employees to have a fun day at the Riverbanks Zoo & Garden in Columbia, South Carolina. At this outing, I met Dr. Anand's wife who was a nice lady, and they met my children. Jaylin, who was now in the tenth grade, loved science, planned to go to college, but did not know what direction to go in her talked with Dr. Anand. We all had a great time getting acquainted with each other.

Columbia SC Zoo

A few days later, I walked into Dr. Anand's office, and he had a chocolate protein power shake and an energy drink on his shelf, so I asked about them. He responded with, "He knew someone that sold them." I also drank protein shakes and energy drinks and wanted something better. When I read the ingredients in his energy drink, I noticed that it was made with quality ingredients, so I bought some chocolate protein powder. When it arrived, I made a shake at home, and it tasted great.

I had always been a firm believer that whether it was a new soldier or in this case a new doctor, I never introduced myself by gossiping about anything negative within the workplace. I strongly believed that people should be given time to form their own thoughts and opinions without the influence of others interfering. I followed this same belief and allowed Dr. Anand to do just that. However, it was not long before our conversations about health transitioned to favoritism and racism amongst students and faculty. As time went by, we became closer. In fact, there was one day when we were talking in his office, and he told me that his sister and brother-in-law were both doctors that lived in California, and they also sold the shakes and energy drinks. He also said that "He spoke with his brother-in-law about Jaylin and I. I said, "Cool." Several weeks later, Dr. Anand told me that his brother-in-law was flying to South Carolina on business, and that he wanted to speak to Jaylin about college and the medical field. So, I asked Jaylin if she was interested, and she agreed to meet with him. That Saturday around 1100 hours, we all met at in the conference room at South University. His brother-in-law seemed like a nice guy, and we talked for hours. He provided Jaylin and I with some helpful information, and we appreciated it.

After our initial meeting, Dr. Anand's brother-in-law and I met at Starbucks. He explained to me how he sold products for a marketing company called Amway. He also talked about Amway's business model and asked, "If I ever thought about owning a business?" I said, "Yes, I wanted to own a health store but not necessarily in that manner." We talked for an hour, and I was not interested, besides, I wanted to learn more about it before committing to anything. I thanked him and I drove home.

I told Quanta what we had discussed, and then I began to read over the pamphlets he gave me. I learned that Amway partnered with companies such as Artistry, Santinique, XS Sports Nutrition and that they also sold quality household, and beauty and health related products. While I was impressed with XS Sports Nutrition, when I learned about a company called Nutrilite, I became excited. They offered quality vitamins and supplements for adults and children, and more importantly, their understanding of quality lined up with what I believed. Nutrilite was transparent and thoroughly explained how they developed and produced their vitamins; the quality of their products was second to none, and I wanted those vitamins for my family and to help others. This was going to be my version of a health store, so I told Dr. Anand that I was interested and became an Amway distributor.

I began learning more about the products and weekly after work, Dr. Anand and I drove to Charlotte, North Carolina to do just that. We met other Amway distributors and talked about our businesses and products. I began listening to cassette disk and reading books about business. I really enjoyed the books that were about personal growth and development. I also began using our products, and although I enjoyed our no sugar energy drinks with natural flavors and vitamins, I did not like half of the protein bars. My family and I used the vitamins and powders that helped with digestive problems, joint pain, lack of fiber, and nutritional deficiencies. The Artistry products were excellent. I started using our skin care products, which were incredible, and I learned so much about my skin type and how to take care of it. The ladies' makeup, lip gloss, antioxidant drink twist tubes, detergent, dishwashing liquid, and hair products were excellent as well.

Dr. Anand's sister and brother-in-law also talked with him and I weekly. They helped us both, and on the day of my grand opening, they flew back to South Carolina and helped me. It was a success, and I appreciated those that supported me, and although my financial success depended upon others becoming distributors, that was not my number one goal. I often thought not only about myself, but also about my friends, family, fellow veterans, and children with who suffered from digestive issues, nutritional deficiencies, were overweight, had chronic joint pain, liver and/or kidney damage, diabetes, acid reflux, cholesterol concerns, acne, nerve damage, menopause concerns and much more. Therefore, I did not care whether someone became a distributor and I rarely spoke with anyone about doing so, because I knew that there were more people like me that needed these vitamins and I wanted to help them.

As I gained love for our products, I also began to hate my job even more. Every day for lunch, I always left the building by myself. I needed time to myself. However, I can remember agreeing to have lunch with a couple of coworkers at a restaurant in town. I was the only Black person in the group of five, and as I sat at the table, there was a well-dressed White man in the restaurant who was constantly looking at me. So, I started to look back at him, and I made it so obvious that the guy I worked for noticed. Afterwards, I felt as if they knew each other and had been talking about me. In April of 2017, I resigned, and truthfully if it were not for my family and Dr. Anand, I would have moved on when the others did.

I continued to sell my products and loved helping my friends and fellow veterans. Everyone that used our products saw some improvement and I was happy for them. On another occasion, my business partners flew to Virginia and helped me with my grand opening. I displayed our products and had great conversations with everyone that attended. I considered it a success and I appreciated their support.

CHAPTER 64

The American Legion

I was also enjoying my time at our American Legion; it was fun, and I was acquainted with some good people. I felt that they believed in me, and I did not want to let them down. I often drove to our bank to make deposits, and I also picked up liquor, food, and other supplies. Our commander and adjutant planned parties and we made money. I saved money, paid our bills, renegotiated payment plans, and created an easy to read but very thorough and transparent finance report. It answered every question anyone had and if it did not, I changed it to do so the following month. After fifteen months, we had increased employees pay, helped children with school supplies, fixed ongoing tax concerns, invested in new appliances and equipment, fixed broken kitchen items (e.g., proper ventilation, air conditioning), passed our health and environmental control inspection, opened the kitchen, and sold food, built a brand new bar, cut down unsightly shrubbery, remodeled the dance floor, and repaired the roof, bathroom, and parking lot.

We were rolling and our commander's vision was coming to fruition. While I was happy about it all, I had been on the go since I had retired from the Army, and by this time I was physically and mentally tired. So, in May of 2017, I resigned from my position and continued to focus on my health.

American Legion Finance Officer

CHAPTER 65

Fort Jackson Postal School

In January of 2018, a job recruiter called me. There was a postal instructor position available at Fort Jackson and he wanted to know if I was interested. I said, "Yes," and drove to the postal school where two men interviewed me. One worked at the school and the other, who managed contractors, had driven down from Richmond, Virginia. They were both veterans. After the interview, they hired me.

I worked with a small group of people that consisted of civilians and service members from the Army, Air Force, and Marines. I first had to complete a two-week course that taught me how to instruct before I could begin teaching. After I completed the course, I returned to the postal school and began to watch and learn from the other instructors. It was a five-week course that taught service members from all branches of the military how to work in a post office. I also began to teach subjects that I understood. During the middle of class, the postal machines and equipment always broke down, and I was always stopping class to either fix or replace something. After I taught a block of instructions, the service members would have to completed practical exercises. Since we graded everything manually, every instructor chipped in when it was time to do so. Then I would conduct a thorough review before passing out the examinations for testing. After we finished grading them, we gave our students their results. The course was rigorous, fast paced, and I had to stand on my feet for hours.

After work, I brought lesson plans home to read. I woke up at 0400 hours to read and review before work. On Saturday mornings, a Marine would let me in the building to practice. I did this weekly, because they had hired me to teach and I wanted to be proficient at my job, so I had to quickly learn the material.

CHAPTER 66

The Recruiting Reunion

One day at work, I was talking to a sergeant that was an Army instructor about instructing and the different challenges we faced. We also talked about football and how she was a huge fan of the UVA football team. She said she was from Charlottesville, Virginia. I told her that "I had recruited in that area." After looking at each other, I smiled and said, "I remember you, I was your recruiter." She remembered me too, turned red and laughed. We hugged and reminisced. I had met her when she was a sophomore in high school. She was a nice student and was interested in joining the Air Force. During her junior and senior years, we continued to talk at school, and after she graduated, I followed up with her, but she was still not ready. Then one day, I followed up with her and she was still not ready, but she also said that "She needed to do something!" If the Air Force recruiter had to recruit, I believe that she would have joined that branch. However, after two years of building trust and repour, she joined the Army. I was happy for her, and the reunion was great.

I continued teaching for other instructors until I had taught every class. Then I received my own class of twenty-five students to teach. I taught Monday through Friday from 0800 hours to 1600 hours, I made mistakes, learned from them, and continued teaching. I done my best and I never wanted a student to fail. However, when a student failed, I had to counsel them in writing, and another instructor would retrain them before I could evaluate them again.

Throughout the week, I often had medical appointments, and while I was at my appointments, other instructors would fill in for me. Once I returned from my appointment, I would take over the class. My students knew I was a new instructor and were patient with me. Although, this was my second time around, teaching was more physically and mentally challenging than it had been before. However, I done the best that I could, but I often made mistakes. In fact, I made so many that I often had to put my class on break to ask for help. Because of my shortcomings, I always ensured that I done a thorough review.

One day during our break, one of my students walked up to me very enthusiastically and said, "Mr. Hicks, has anyone ever told you that you sound like Denzel Washington in the movie *Training Day*?" I laughed, said "Yes, and I'm a huge fan of his." After five long weeks, my students graduated. The graduation ceremony was nice and professionally done, and I was happy for them and happy to see them leave. It had been exhausting.

I continued filling in wherever I was needed, prior to being assigned my second class to teach. The days following my assignment, the physical and mental workload began to take its toll on me. There were mornings that I had to call out. I had not been sleeping well and the thoughts of making a mistake in class kept my anxiety through the roof. In addition, the sergeant I had put in the Army was a daily reminder of my recruit that had died in Afghanistan.

I began to call out more frequently and my supervisor did not like it, and one day, after I had called out the guy from Richmond called me. He asked me, "What was going on?" and I explained to him why I could not work. After our conversation, he told me that he was a retired Army command sergeant major and then he talked about his troubles and how he managed them. Then he bluntly said to me, "You need to get your sh$$ together." I said, "OKAY, Sir" and hung up the phone. After talking with Quanta, in June of 2018, I took his advice and respectfully resigned. After my resignation, I continued with my physical therapy, chiropractic, and mental health appointments.

Postal Instructor - Mr. Hicks

CHAPTER 67

Racial Profiling 2019

October 10, 2019, I drove from South Carolina to Florida to visit Kendrick, and some of my friends from JDUB in Portsmouth also drove down. When we had all arrived safely, we partied for three days, and it was fun and good to see everyone. Early that Sunday morning, we all drove to Miami to see the Washington Redskins verse the Miami Dolphins football game and it was a great game with Washington winning by one point. On the morning of October 14, 2019, my friends woke up at 0400 hours to drive back to Portsmouth. I told them all goodbye and laid back down until 0700 hours. Afterwards, Kendrick and I drove back to his house, and we went for a walk. Then I told him that "I had to go," and said, "Goodbye." Before I drove off, I made sure my license and registration were in my cup holder.

When I reached the Jacksonville, Florida area, the interstate changed to four lanes. And since I was tired and not in a rush, I rode in the far righthand lane behind an eighteen-wheeler truck. Everything was fine, until I crossed the Georgia state line. Within ten minutes of me entering the state, I looked into my rearview mirror and noticed a police car approximately thirty yards in the left-hand lane behind me. I said to myself, "Here we go again." I continued driving behind the truck and never switched lanes. A few moments later, the police car swiftly cut across one lane and drove off the interstate ramp.

Two minutes later, another police car appeared and began to follow me. When the police officer cut on his police lights, I rolled all my windows down, grabbed my credentials, placed both hands directly on my steering wheel, and pulled over. My hands remained on the steering wheel, as the officer quickly exited his car and walked to the passenger side of my car. He asked for my license and registration. I gave it to him as well as my military identification card. He asked me "If I knew why he pulled me over?" and I said, "No sir." He then said, "I was swerving and following the truck to close, and that I had to remain two car lengths behind the truck." Then the police officer turned and walked back to his car to check my license. As I waited in my car, I knew he was lying. He had pulled me over because I was Black, wore a New York Mets shirt, and drove a Honda Accord with New York tags thru the state of Georgia. I had been profiled as a drug trafficker before they pulled me over.

In the arm rest of my rental car was a small jar with less than two grams of marijuana in it. The police officer may have smelled it, and now that he had seen my gold teeth, and twisted hair, I fit the description.

The officer returned to my car and asked me to step out. When I exited my car, the police officer asked, "Where is the weed at I smell it." I told him "I had a small jar with less than two grams in my arm rest, because I suffered from chronic PTSD and needed it." He told me to place my hands over my head and he searched me. As he searched me, another police car arrived. Once he finished his search of me, he walked me to the back of my rental car. Once we reached the back of my car, he looked at me and said, "Well what about this?" He pointed at my rear bumper as if I had drugs stashed there. I said, "Sir I do not see anything wrong with the bumper. This is a rental car, and I did not touch the bumper." He asked me where I was driving from. I said, "Sir I am driving from Miami. I was there for a football game. He then said, "Oh yeah well who was playing." As he removed my Washington Redskins blanket that was made in South Korea from the trunk, I said, "Sir, it was the Redskins verse the Dolphins." He then asked me "Who won?," and I said, "Washington won 17-16."

As he began to search my car, I stood in front of his police car and behind my rental car. Seconds later, two other big police officers walked towards me. They were obviously not comfortable with me standing there so they placed me in handcuffs. As the police officer done this, he asked me, "So do you live in South Carolina?" I said "Yes, Sir!" Then he asked me the amount of marijuana I had, and I said, "Sir it's just a little bit." He asked me "If it was an ounce?" and I said, "No, Sir!" He then asked me "If it was legal in South Carolina." I said, "No, sir." He walked me to the back of the police car and sat me in the back seat. The police officer searching my car found a plastic bag with something black in it. He yelled back to one of the other police officers for me to provide an explanation. When he opened the car door, I yelled, "Sir it is black soap. I use it to wash my face."

Moments later, a police officer removed me from the car and removed the handcuffs. Their facial expressions told it all, and they looked like idiots. The officer handed me my jar and told me to pour it out. As I done so, the two officers walked off and I was there with the officer who had conducted the search. Officer Martin looked at me and said, "Thanks for telling me the truth. If this is something you need, keep it in your house, and understand that we have a job to do." I nodded north and south, grabbed my warning ticket for swerving and following too close and walked to my car. I drove off and made it safely back to South Carolina.

CHAPTER 68

What Gave Me the Idea and Why Did I Do This?

One day while I was in therapy, we were discussing ways to deal with stress. I had previously tried a variety of things such as praying, exercising, changing my diet, alcohol, reading, and meditation, but none of it had worked. When my therapist suggested journaling and how it was a way to remove negative thoughts out of my head by writing it down on paper, I considered it. And I had too. I carried an enormous amount of anger inside of me and I wanted and needed to stop thinking about the things that angered me the most. This has helped.

Plus, I wanted my children to know more about me.

CHAPTER 69

My Life Today - 2024

Quanta and I have now been married for twenty-eight years. I love Quanta and our marriage is stronger today than it has ever been.

Jaylin majored in biology and graduated from Clemson University. She is currently working and studying for medical school. Her plans are to become an anesthesiologist and her hair is still natural and healthy.

Kyra is doing well and loves middle school. As a six grader, Kyra was ranked number three out of a class of three hundred and seven students. As a seventh grader, her core classes are all accelerated. Up to this point, she has A's with an occasional B. Kyra is also a second-degree black belt and will earn her third-degree black belt Apr of 2024. She teaches Taekwondo at a local middle school and earns a wage for doing so. She has taken part and won taekwondo tournaments from as far out as Las Vegas. She has also taught herself how to read and write in Korean. Lastly, Kyra loves to play the piano and has performed in three recitals. We are proud of our children.

Thanks for reading!

CONGRATS!
JAYLIN